Prima Donna Sunshine

Marlaina Donato

Prima Donna Sunshine

Prima Donna Sunshine
Copyright ©2012 Marlaina Donato
All Rights Reserved

ISBN-13: 978-1470078355
ISBN-10: 147007835X

Design by Marlaina Donato

Prima Donna Sunshine

Also by the same author

Naked Soul

A Brief Infinity

The Silver Ladder

Prima Donna Sunshine

Author's note:

For reasons of privacy and creative license,
names and locations have been changed,
and some characters and events are composite.

Prima Donna Sunshine

For my Mother
for giving me beauty, breath, and purpose-
and for the infinite capacity
of her heart, even when love was blind.

And for Molly, who can finally see
the buttercup's reflection.

Prima Donna Sunshine

Share your light
Prima Donna Sunshine
What you are
Always be what you are
My mystic star
Be who you are
Don't let the world
Try to make you over
Just shine for me
Always free

-Emma Dorman
"Prima Donna Sunshine"

1

She reminds me of an old-fashioned Valentine; she has the same blushing high cheek bones and hair swirled on top of her head. She passes our house every day around four o'clock, and she's the most beautiful woman I have ever seen. She wears crimson running clothes and looks too proper to even break a sweat. I wait for a glimpse of her as I watch *The Golden Girls* re-runs and wait on pins and needles for Daddy's car and the sound of the garage door creaking open.

I observe her through every window of the house as she jogs along the street past our driveway and onto the main road. The rain puddle just before the stop sign catches her reflection, and then she is out of sight. Sometimes watching her makes my heart beat as fast as a hummingbird's wings.

Sometimes four o'clock is the only thing I get out of bed for.

That and my old manual typewriter. Every letter sounds like someone cracking gum as I try to crank out fifteen pages a day, sometimes twenty. I don't know who will publish a novel written by a sixteen-year-old girl, but I'll cross that bridge when I come to The End, whenever that will be. My Aunt Dot calls from Brooklyn and asks, "Molly, aren't you finished with that book yet?" I tell her that Margaret Mitchell took ten years to write *Gone with the Wind*. That usually satisfies her until the next phone call.

Dorian, Brian, Linda, Tawny, and Julie are my characters, and I know them by heart. To me, words are like warm clay; I can create worlds by molding them together. Most of all, I can create a world where I feel more at home. Sometimes the people who live on my pages are more alive than the people around me.

Except for Lance. I saw him again the other night. He came by to drop off some demos for Mama. He plays guitar and has hair black as India ink. He looks like a Siberian husky with those eyes the color of ice. He's the only one in this stupid town worth daydreaming about. But he has a girlfriend, and I have books to write and canvases to paint.

And besides, I'm saving myself for Neil Diamond. I have every record he ever released, British imports, and his personal assistant's home phone number. Someday he's going to sing my mother's songs, and then she can get out of that job. We'll leave New Jersey and move to California. We'll buy Daddy that sailboat he's been dreaming of. He'll stop boozing. We'll have a good life.

He comes home sober, but within two hours his face looks like a bruised tomato, and he slurs the two words he says to me on his way through the kitchen. I'm invisible as the furniture as I chop and dice, season and stir. I try to cook something wonderful every night, but Daddy's already two sheets to the wind by the time Mama gets home from work around eight. I want Daddy to notice how clean the house is and to say, "The dinner smells good." But he just grumbles that something stinks and to put on the exhaust fan.

He threatens to kick our dog Schnapps if he barks to get his attention. It's my job to put the dog in my room when Daddy first comes home so he won't be bothered. It makes me crazy when he tries to kick Schnapps in the ribs and yells, "Get outta here, you black fuck!" I scream at him to stop, but I really want to kick Daddy right back to let him know what it's like.

Our poor Schnapps—my Baby Love. Part black Labrador and poodle, he looks like a curly Benji with a copper mustache. We got him when I was eleven. He took to Daddy right away and leaned his head on Daddy's shoulder all the way home. He came with the name Snooper, but we changed it to Schnapps after he drank some of Daddy's beer. Now he barks frantically for his attention then cowers just in case the kick comes.

I want to get Daddy's attention, too, but I figure I should just leave him alone. He has a long road to hoe, so Mama says. He has a frozen knee from botched surgery long before I was born, yet he drives the Boscos to their penthouse at the Essex House in Manhattan, cleans their indoor pool, keeps the estate grounds tidy, and punctuates everything with "Yes, Mr. and Mrs. B."

Mama's official title at the Bosco estate is Mrs. B's personal assistant and housekeeper. I don't know how Mama doesn't strangle that old bitch.

Mrs. B pinched my cheek when I was at the estate last week and then flashed that alligator grin and said, "Molly, you're such a sweet, pretty girl. But don't you wish you didn't have such a fat ass?"

"I do, actually," I answered with a laugh and left before she saw my face crack with tears.

Yeah, I have a bit of a fat ass. Maybe it's teenage hormones. Maybe it's my fate. I remind myself that I'm working on it as I peddle my bike down the road around four o'clock. I look up, and there she is, Beautiful Lady, panting loud enough to be audible as she jogs up the incline past the dry creek bed. "Hi," I manage to croak in a half-whisper, barely able to look her in the eyes. Green eyes, like mine. She smiles in response and keeps going. I peddle to the end of the road, and the loneliness inside my chest rises up like a tsunami. I lost touch with my friends once I quit school. It would be nice to have a real friend.

Sometimes I wonder who the bullies will shove up against the wall now that the girl with the hook nose is gone. I wonder who else is getting death threats by those girls who wear knuckle rings and keep vodka in their lockers and no one does anything about it.

Mama had a fit when I told her I wanted to quit school this past spring. I told her that I'd rather be dead than take another day of it and that I'd get my GED. Daddy sided with me, and I quit two months before tenth grade was over.

When The Old Bitch heard about the bullying, she offered to pay for a nose job if I want it. Mama says that a lot of geniuses in history had a nose like mine, with a bump on the bridge. I guess I'm in good company. I don't know about the genius aspect, but maybe it won't hurt if I look the part.

People say I should get a job, but my parents say that they'd rather have me help out and hold up the house while they cater to The Old Bitch and her passive husband. Our house, two doors down from the Boscos, goes with my parents' job, so I guess we'll be here in New Blair until Neil Diamond calls.

I enjoy making a home. Two years ago I took a nanny's position in London for a month and loved it. I worked for a film producer, a friend of The Old Bitch. I cooked, tidied their four-bedroom flat, and took care of three kids.

Sometimes I actually believe this house is a real home. It looks like it on the surface—Mama's numerous colored glass jars light up like church windows when the sun pours into the kitchen, and our living room is warm and inviting with a console piano and Daddy's handmade bookcases. My bedroom has a writing desk, an easel and drafting table, and prints from Picasso's Blue Period.

But somewhere deep inside, I know the truth. It's like a monster I try to ignore and push down the drain. It wakes me in the middle of the night and makes me shake until I almost throw up.

Daddy will never stop drinking. Mama may even die before him. Maybe I'll just kill myself if there's no other way out. Hey, Hemingway did it. Van Gogh did it. Sara Teasdale, my favorite poet, did it. Maybe some people are born just to set themselves on fire.

Maybe I'm one of them.

Gold leaves drift like confetti along the roadsides, and the air is tinged with fires and decay. It's October, my favorite month of the year. It's the only time I'm not squirming to get out of New Blair. The farm stands sell pumpkins, apples, and Indian corn. Twenty minutes away, just over the Pennsylvania border, there's a farm that sells fifteen different kinds of apples and five kinds of pears that I put to good use.

I've been baking up a storm. Like Mama, I love to cook. She doesn't have time anymore, so the kitchen has become second nature to me. Right now our yellow kitchen counter is overflowing with muffins and quick breads. The scent of cinnamon and apples seems to make it feel as if everything's normal around here.

I'm still working on the Fat Ass Project, riding my bike, and dancing in the living room. I don't know what good it does because after I come back inside, after passing Beautiful Lady, I bury my head in bowls of hot chicken noodle soup and those muffins. After I stuff myself, I sit down at my typewriter to write a chapter or two and try to ignore the fact that my ass feels even fatter than it did two hours earlier.

Speaking of writing, I met a science fiction writer at church last Sunday. He was pasty and drooled at the corners of his mouth, but I was anxious to hear about his work. He stuffed his face with a brownie, and asked, "So, what are you writing, *Purple Passion*?" Crumbs rocketed out past the drool on the last two syllables. I proceeded to give him an answer beyond his intellectual capacity, and he walked away knowing that this sixteen-year-old girl has more to write about than heaving bosoms.

Not that I have much experience with bosoms. My breasts look like mosquito bites on steroids, and one is smaller than the other. I avoid the mirror at all costs. There's nothing I can do about it but hope that Mother Nature balances things out over the next couple of years.

I can, though, do something about this mop of boring brown hair. I can't believe my grandmothers on both sides of the family were flaming redheads, and I got stuck with dull brown. I soak it in lemon juice and sit outside in the sun for hours until my head is stiff as shellac. It only gives me copper highlights, but it's better than shit brown. I'm going to buy some henna, leave it on for three hours and see how that turns out. Mama will probably kill me if it turns out Lucille Ball red, but I'll just blame it on misjudgment of time.

Beautiful Lady has auburn hair, just enough red in the brown to match some of the leaves out there. She says "hello" to me now when we pass each other near the dry creek bed. I pretend to have my mind on other things and look up the last second to respond. I wonder what her name is, where she lives, and if she was ever a model.

Once in a while, Renee from my old Social Studies class stops by. She gibbers about losing her virginity and papering her wall with fashion clippings and posters of that singer Madonna. She tells me she forces herself to throw up after she eats so she won't get fat. She also has a pot plant at her friend's house, and they smoke together and talk about their boyfriends. Renee likes Greek mythology and writes poetry, so I guess that's why we're friends, well, sort of.

I'm on page one hundred of my book. I don't know how good it is, but Mama reads my work every night after she comes in, no matter how tired she is. She says it's the highlight of her day. That and our talks after Daddy goes to bed. Sometimes we make Earl Grey in her favorite Chinese tea pot and talk about everything. She's my best friend. She has been since I was nine and she sat me down to tell me she had breast cancer. She survived, but I never took another moment with her for granted.

Sometimes it feels like it's Mama and me against the

world. We've weathered more storms than we can count. Nothing else matters as long as we have each other. I just wish she didn't have to work so hard and that she had more time for her music. She and Lance want to record more songs, but I don't know when that's going to happen.

Sometimes I worry myself sick about both my parents. Doing something beautiful in the house usually gets my mind off my anxieties.

I fixed up the house again this week. I moved around some furniture, put up the new curtains, and put down new rugs in Mama and Daddy's bathroom. The new shades of burgundy weren't on the floor long enough to even be walked on before Daddy got so drunk that he got the shits and puked all over the bathroom. He staggered to bed ranting that I'm lazy and a worthless lard ass.

It's nothing new. I just try to laugh with sarcasm and think that it's getting to be almost a term of endearment, just without the fuzzy feeling.

I guess it could be worse. Mama grew up so poor that she used newspaper for toilet paper and starved for days at a time after her father died and her Mom went on binges. I guess Home Sweet Home isn't sweet, anywhere.

Sometimes I wonder about Zane, my biological father. I wonder if he's still violent and if he regrets letting my mother go. He was a genius, Mama says, a painter, with the notorious bump on the bridge of the nose. I think about him most when I'm drawing portraits, when my pastels blend into colors even more beautiful than I had intended. I wonder if he ever thinks about me.

Our neighbor who shares our driveway and lives two houses back strolled to get her mail today with her usual walking stick for support. She's old and stout and sour as a crabapple because Daddy gives her dirty looks when she passes our house. He calls her The Stick. She wanted to make friends with us when we moved in three years ago, but now she dislikes all of us, even me. I try to smile at her and be nice, but it's no use.

The people next door have a brood, and each one has wiry copper hair. The girl, close to my age, stood outside under the maples this past May while everyone snapped pictures of her before she left for the prom. I hate school and think proms are insipid, but I felt envious of her, dressed in a gown the color of rubies. Her father wasn't drunk, and things appeared as normal as normal can be.

We have moments of normal, too, mostly on Sundays when we go to a non-denominational church. Mama brushes out her shoulder-length chestnut hair and wears a red rose pin on her blouse. Her beautiful profile reminds me of an antique cameo. Daddy wears a Navy blue blazer, winks at me with a sober smile and pretends to be singing along to the hymns. The lady who plays the organ is a volunteer and hasn't progressed much through the years. Daddy nudges me and whispers, "Nedda's got the boxing gloves on again." We try not to wince when she makes a blunder, but it's hard.

Mike, a kid my age, goes to church with his mother. He says he's in love with me, even though we have never said more than two sentences to each other. His mother chews gum during the service and wears miniskirts and hot pink flowers in her hair. When Mama asked her about her new job, Mike's Mom answered with a smile, "Let's just say it's what I do best." She winked and then dropped the subject.

Thanksgiving is approaching soon, and I dread the holidays. Another year we'll have to eat out because Daddy will have to drive the Boscos to their relatives. They pay for our meal, but I'd much rather cook us a feast at home. Daddy doesn't care, and it makes me furious. Just as well, though, that he works on that day. That means he'll be sober, and things will be more like they used to be.

Daddy and I were once buddies. We looked for fossils, and he taught me the name of every tree on our property in Pennsylvania. We sat on our old porch swing and listened to the madrigals of the birds until twilight turned.

I miss those days when we lived in the Poconos, but they were a long time ago. Daddy can still be sweet, bring home a surprise from the book store or art shop—new pastels or something—but he hasn't really looked at me since I grew out of the cutesy years.

The other day he mentioned my "blue" eyes. "Daddy, my eyes are not blue. What color are my eyes?" I asked.

"If they're not blue, they're brown."

"Nope."

"Then they're gray, like your mother's."

"Nope."

"Then what to hell color are they?"

"Green. Never mind." And that's how it goes.

Last night I dreamed that Daddy, Mama and I were swimming through a bog. We were half afloat and nearly drowning as we tried to reach land in the darkness. It felt like an eternity until I finally reached a grassy bank. Then the scene changed, and I was a lot older; I was an artist, and I lived in the Southwest like Georgia O' Keeffe. My paintings vibrated with color and covered the walls in every room of the house. And I had red hair. I never did find out what happened to Mama and Daddy in the bog.

Dreams are weird. Sometimes life is weirder. I can't figure out any of it, so for now, the Fat Ass Project is paramount, and I am determined to befriend Beautiful Lady sometime before Christmas. I have a personal deadline.

2

Daddy drives me to the store to buy some groceries. As usual, he waits in the car so he can nip some booze. I figure it's better than the times he comes in with me and grabs handfuls of cookies from the bulk bins and chows down right in front of pretending-to-be-oblivious shoppers. Lady Luck and the Patron Saint of Losers must be working on my case overtime because on my way out of the store, I notice Beautiful Lady going in. I rush into the car with the grocery bags and lie through my teeth to Daddy that I've forgotten something. Happily half-lit, he tells me to take my time.

I run back into the store so fast I almost trip over my shoes and manage to pull myself together in time to track her down by the chicken cutlets. I walk nonchalantly down the meat aisle and take an unprecedented die-hard interest in Cornish game hens.

Sooner than later, we're face to face. I try to act casual. "Hi," she offers, smiling. She's even more beautiful up close; she's so beautiful that I feel ugly and fat. And short. She must be five foot ten with a body like an Ertè sculpture. "Ah, hi... you look familiar. You're the lady who jogs, right?" I say.

"That's right. You're the girl on the bike."

"Do you like running? I'm thinking of trying it, but I don't know." I swallow hard and thank God I'm not Pinocchio.

"I think you would like it. Hey, if you wanna come along with me sometime, feel free to give it a shot. I wouldn't mind the company."

"Yeah?"

"It gets a little boring by myself."

"Ah, sure. I'll try it. Riding the bike gets monotonous. When?"

"I would like to stay on track with exercise even though the holidays are coming. I'll be running on Christmas Eve, but you'll probably be busy."

"No, I'm free..."

"3:15 or so- we don't get back in the dark. Where do you live?"

"The tan ranch house just before the stop sign, the one with the big maple by the mailbox."

"I'll meet you in front of your house."

"Sounds good."

"By the way, my name is Catharine. Call me Kate."

"I'm Molly."

"Take care, Molly."

"Thanks. See ya then." I saunter down another aisle, grab a can of Campbell's mushroom soup to purchase as my "forgotten" item and refrain from attempting a Baryshnikov leap. Then I realize I'd better buy running shoes and be prepared to make an ass out of myself.

Before I know it, December is almost over, and Mama's fervent intention of finding time or energy to prepare for Christmas just doesn't pan out. I put up the tree, and I'll probably take it down after New Year's, too. Part of me hates the whole thing all together because I know that Mama and Daddy will be working through the holidays.

The Old Bitch doesn't believe in Christmas, but she makes my mother put up a Christmas tree in the solarium next to the indoor pool on the far side of the house. That way her intellectual, atheist friends won't see it. When one or two catch on, she blames it on her husband and her "simple-minded housekeeper."

Actually, The Old Bitch shuns the dogma of any orthodox religion and is addicted to New Age philosophies. She goes to a psychic regularly who tells her that she was everyone from Cleopatra to Joan of Arc in previous lifetimes. She pays me twenty bucks to type two hours of recorded readings every month and gets her knickers in a knot if I am a couple days late with the assignment. The problem is that it takes four hours to complete. I play, rewind, play, rewind and hope I heard right. The psychic sounds like he's talking in tongues through a mouthful of crunchy peanut butter. I try hard not to roll my eyes because that alone will set me back three sentences and then it's play, rewind, play, rewind, *curse*.

Sometimes when I'm at the estate, her teeth begin to chatter wildly. She informs me that Emmanuel, her spirit guide, is afoot somewhere in the house because that's what happens each time he pays her a visit. She's an amateur sculptor, but I think she missed her calling and should have been on the stage. She created a statue of Emmanuel and put it in a shrine opposite the side door. Mama has to make sure it's cleaned and that Mrs. B's daily offerings of flowers and plants stay fresh. Frankly, I think The Old Bitch is so open-minded that her brain fell out. Not that I don't believe in spirits and angels. I've seen a few in my time. I just know bullshit when I smell it.

Mr. B is a sweet soul, twenty-one years older than The Old Bitch. He is distinguished with his full head of silky, white hair and his tapered mustache. He composes improv classical music every morning on their grand piano and barely speaks above a whisper. He's a self-made millionaire, in the steel industry, and still goes to work most days of the week. Rumor has it that at age eighty-eight he has a side dish, a secretary. Daddy is instructed to drive Mr. B to see her off-hours but knows nothing of the details. All I know is that if The Old Bitch ever found out, Mr. B's white head would go rolling down their cedar-lined driveway like a bowling ball.

I wrapped presents, made my annual chocolate-laced eggnog for the Boscos, and made a turkey dinner that we'll eat at some point on this Christmas Eve, after Mama and Daddy get out of jail sometime after nine. The Old Bitch wants me to stop by as I always do on Christmas Eve. I have to find something in the closet that masks my failure at The Fat Ass Project or she might bring up the subject in front of her guests.

I stop farting around when I realize that it's almost time to meet Kate. I scramble to get dressed. Despite the crazy, unseasonable temperature of seventy degrees, I pull on burgundy sweat pants that make my butt feel like a bratwurst. I lace up sneakers and throw on my Navy blue hooded sweat jacket and glance out the window. I see Kate near our driveway stretching in place gracefully as a ballerina at the barre while she checks her watch. I'm ready to fly out the door when the zipper on my jacket gets stuck. It won't budge. Kate checks her watch once more and looks toward the house before she continues her run, obviously mistaken I am not going with her after all. I curse, give the zipper one last tug and sigh relief when it finally zips up.

I run out to the street waving a like a lunatic. "Kate, wait up!" I sprint to the stop sign and explain I had been detained the last minute. She assumes it's frantic holiday stuff. I go along with it.

And then we start running. She shows me how to place my arms and gives me tips about breathing and posture. We talk as we make our way down the two lane highway, and by the time we reach the second house past the Bosco's driveway, I am winded as a cow doing aerobics. I keep trudging on so she doesn't think I'm a wimp and focus on what she tells me.

Her last name is Hall. She lives at the mountainous end of Anderson Road. She's married to a guy named Jake who likes writing plays and hunting deer. She has three boys, ages twelve to seventeen. She's a private, professional caregiver and no, she was never a model. Like me, she quit school.

I tell her I'm writing a book and that I help my parents out the best I can. The setting sun drops a blinding gold curtain ahead of us, and she says she must remind herself to wear sunglasses next time. She asks me how I'm doing, if I need to stop for a bit. By now my legs are past pain and into stage two numb, but I'll be damned if I don't go the distance. She says once we reach the mile and a half mark, we'll stop and walk back to my house.

We agree to run again after Christmas. Once I'm in the house I crash on the couch fearing I might cough up a lung, but I know that I did it. Not just running a mile and a half the first time out, but befriending Beautiful Lady, I mean Kate Hall.

Christmas Eve is turning out okay. Daddy has only a little snoot-full, too little to be noticed by the Boscos and their guests. I stand most of the time with my back to something solid so The Old Bitch can't dissect me.

Her nephew Rob bows like a gentleman and introduces himself. I laugh, and we shake hands. He's tall and skinny like Fred Astaire with soulful blue eyes. He says he just got back from an ashram in India. He's the black sheep of the family, exchanging skills for tools of enlightenment. Gourmet vegetarian cooking is his forte. He offers me a homemade chocolate truffle. It melts in my mouth the way I imagine Neil Diamond or Lance kissing me, and I want to know more about Rob's meditation pilgrimages.

I notice The Old Bitch across the room smiling like a hyena when she sees us talking. I think she wants to set us up, fat ass and all. Rob must be ten to twelve years older than me, but something in his manner makes him appear older. An old soul, I guess.

Well, things are looking up. Kate Hall and Rob Bosco noticed my existence. My fat ass didn't make it into the conversation, and Daddy was civil. 1986 just might come in on a beautiful note.

Interstate 80, normally a crazy and sometimes treacherous highway, is even more dangerous when Dad's at the wheel. Unbeknownst to Mama and me, he tanked up on booze right before we left the house. Halfway to the mall, the effects are perfectly clear. He's drunk as a skunk.

Cars behind us are honking as Dad's speed slows down to forty miles an hour. Down to thirty-five. Cars are now storming by, and drivers press middle fingers to the windows. "Tom, pull over...pull over now! You're going to get us killed. You were drinking," Mama yells.

"Ah, shut up. I'm fine. Let 'em all go by, sons-of-bitches."

"Tom, come on, give me the keys."

"Ah, who the hell's 'rinkin'? Nobody's 'rinkin'." He swerves over the yellow line more times than I can count, and I look out the back window for cops. None yet. I just hope to Hell we get where we're going before Dad crashes the car, gets arrested, or gets sick.

I throw off my earphones and toss my Walkman. By now I'm yelling from the back seat, and my voice goes up at least an octave. "Dad, for chrissake, pull over! You can't drive! You don't wanna lose your license!"

"Shut that friggin' kid up, will ya, Emma?"

"Tom, pull over!" Mama tries again, touching the wheel to maybe scare him into pulling onto the side of the highway.

"Dad, come on!"

"Shut up, you little bitch." A tractor trailer bears down on our bumper, and my heart feels like it will go through my chest.

After what feels like enough time to live, die, and be reincarnated, we're finally at a stop, parked in front of Macy's. Mama turns around to look at me with misty eyes, grabs my hand, and lets out a sigh of relief. She then grabs the keys from the ignition and informs The-One-Who's-Not-'Rinkin' that she will be driving home. "Fuck you. I'm stayin' here," he says.

"Good!" Mama yells back, getting out of the car. "Sleep

it off." She slams the car door, and he mumbles under his breath, "Motherfucker." I get out of the car and slam my door, too. I slam it louder than Mama slammed hers, just because I know he hates it. I can read his lips through the glass, "Motherfuckers." Oh goody. He makes it plural so I won't feel left out.

With our legs shaking from adrenaline, Mama and I go into the mall arm in arm. I try to take my mind off everything by perusing the poster shop while Mama makes a stop at the health food store. I buy another Picasso print and a new one of Baryshnikov. I get offended, as always, when I can't find any Neil Diamond posters.

Mama returns with a sad smile and a carob candy bar that we share while we sit on one of the benches. We watch people walk by, but we're both in a daze. It's been a rough nine months.

One day back in April, Mama and I couldn't find Dad anywhere. The Boscos were staying at their place in the city, so Dad was tanking up on booze more regularly. We searched all over and finally found him in the company Jeep, still in the garage, slumped over the passenger seat in a stupor. Mama tapped his face until he came to, and I thanked God he wasn't dead.

I turned seventeen in June, but as usual we did nothing. Every year I want to have a party, but I really have no one to invite. And besides, I can't count on Dad being sober.

During the summer, the Boscos vacationed at their house in Switzerland for two and a half weeks. Before they left, they handed my parents a laundry list of annual chores. Right before going to the airport, The Old Bitch said, "Have a wonderful vacation, Dears." Yeah, right. Would that vacation be after the driveways are re-paved, the pool drained and re-painted, three cars inspected and cleaned to spotless inside and out, the guest cabin maintained, and the million and one solarium plants watered every other day? Oh, I forgot the driveways and courtyard cleared of all fallen cedar needles. Excuse me, I mean *vacuumed* clear of all fallen cedar needles. As in hand-held vacuum. Give me a break.

Mama's been looking for a new job in every newspaper from here to North Carolina, preferably another private position with more human hours and less responsibility. There was one in Asheville, North Carolina that sounded wonderful. The house went with the job, and they sounded like really nice people. They were even interested in having me teach art to their two young children. But Dad's been so erratic and walking the edge, Mama turned down an interview. We can't go anywhere or uproot with him boozing like this.

It's getting really hard hiding it from the Boscos, our few friends, and neighbors. Dad still manages to keep it together and not drink when he drives The Old Bitch to her sculpting class or the Bosco's penthouse in the city. But aside from that, it's Pandora's Box once he takes that first sip when he gets home. It doesn't help that there's a liquor store so close to our house that we can see the sign from the front lawn.

It's too depressing to think about, so I spend most of my free time writing, drawing, and walking with Kate. We both decided to give up running once our knees started hurting, so we walk every other day and talk about life. She tells me that she and her husband are not doing well and they may divorce. She's never loved him.

I talk about my writing and my parent's job. She doesn't know too much about Dad's problem, but she doesn't care for him at all. He doesn't care for her, either.

One day I couldn't find the right thing to wear to go walking, and he said to Mama, "What's she making a fuss about? She's only going for a walk. I think she's got a crush on that bitch." I heard him on my way into the bathroom, and I almost choked. A crush? Is he insane? How dare he think such a thing!

"Tom, leave her alone. She's seventeen years old. Girls fuss about their clothes."

"I don't know. There's somethin' there."

"Ssh. Shut up," Mama whispered. I quickly found what I wanted to wear and flew out the door before he could see my face burning up.

God, that's all I need. I have enough on my plate without worrying if I'm really a lesbian. I mean, I never wanted to kiss a girl in my life.

When I was thirteen, I had heard about someone who was gay, and I prayed it would never happen to me. I couldn't imagine anything worse than being into girls.

Well, maybe being a perv. That's the worst of all. But "gay" is definitely bad enough.

Back in junior high, there was an annoying girl who talked too much and buzzed around me like a fly around watermelon. She'd come up behind me and slap me on the rear whenever I was putting books into my locker or walking out to the bus. The other girls warned me to stay away from "her kind." I didn't know exactly what they meant by that. Her kind. Girls who talk too much? Or give you little presents for no reason? That didn't sound like a crime to me. And hey, what's a slap on the rear? It was better than having a grungy boy do it. Well, I guess.

God, I can't be gay. Or worse, what if I'm AC/DC? I love men, older men, that is. I have to be normal. No one in our family is gay or whatever shades of gay there might be. I had crushes on boys in kindergarten. In fourth grade, I couldn't get to sleep at nights thinking about Johnny Shelley with the blue eyes and infectious sense of humor. I signed off my virginity to Mr. Neil Leslie Diamond sometime in this lifetime, hopefully sooner than later. I still have terrible, wicked fantasies about Mr. Harrison, my high school music and drama teacher with the dark hair, bedroom eyes, and bad attitude. My eyes spin in my head after I see Lance. I kind of felt a flutter when Rob Bosco talked to me last Christmas.

I want to make mad, passionate love with a man, on a rainy night with the windows open, like Linda, a character in the book I'm writing. I can't be gay.

Speaking of sex, Mama came home laughing the other

day. She told me that someone in Mr. B's company has to take time off from work, maybe even weeks. She's limping around like a crab with back pain because she fell off the bed while in the act. The woman makes no effort to hide the details of the actual events.

There. That's what I want. I wanna hump my brains out, fall off the bed, go on sick leave and let the world know that *I am not gay*.

Well, at least I no longer have a fat ass or shit brown hair. I mixed raw henna powder with hot water until it was the preferred greenish-brown consistency of diarrhea and then coated every strand of hair and left it on for two and a half hours. It took twenty minutes to wash out, and the bathroom looked like a pig farm had exploded by the time I finished. Every time I perspire or get my hair wet, my head smells like musty hay. It's dark auburn, red enough that last week a stranger referred to me as a redhead. Hallelujah. I no longer have a fat ass. I have red hair. And I am not gay.

It's also fact that I have received my first portrait commission from a lady I met at church. She wants me to do pastel paintings of her two dogs. Two hundred bucks. I'd be happier if we didn't get the tragic news about my sometimes-friend Renee. Her step-father killed himself last week, shot his brains out. No one knows why.

Dad knew the man only by acquaintance, never liked him. Upon hearing the news, I was preparing dinner, holding a blue bowl with a flower painted at the bottom. "He was a no-good bum. To hell with him, the worthless bastard," Dad said, with a few in him but sober for the most part. Rage welled up inside me from out of the blue, and I screamed back, "Shut up! You don't know what you're talking about! What did you ever do in your life? Maybe you're the one who should have died!" I threw the bowl against the cabinet so hard that it splintered into pieces and shot into the hallway.

"Molly!" Mama hissed when she heard my response, and then to Dad, "Tom, you don't mean that. What are you becoming?" I bent down and picked out the shards in the hallway carpet as I sobbed uncontrollably.

"That's all right. I'll be gone soon," Dad mumbled. I remained in the hallway, holding the broken splinters. I tried not to cut myself, but a part of me wanted to punish myself for saying such a horrible thing to my father. Mama knelt down and held me, crying into my hair.

We choked down dinner while we watched some mindlessness on the television and then talked about small things—grocery lists, the Boscos, the coming rain while inside I wanted to be somewhere else. Anywhere else. Maybe in an ashram with Rob or somewhere in California watching the sun go down.

Or maybe in Kate's arms, after all.

3

"That's the best thing I ever ate," Dad said tonight after wiping the plate clean. He says that every time when he's in a good mood. I appreciate it. I've been polishing some of my recipes lately and getting paid by Mary, the lady who cleans the Bosco estate, for baking her cupcakes every Saturday. I rarely use white flour, try to keep it healthy, but Mary wants her cupcakes whiter than white or pretty colors. Her favorite are my pink cupcakes sweetened with confectioner's sugar, flavored with lemon and filled with just a bite of strawberry jam.

I've also been writing up a storm. Kate said that she and her husband Jake wanted to read a few chapters. I was thrilled. I gave them my most significant work. I was secretly hoping that Jake would say I have talent and Kate would be impressed.

A couple of weeks ago, Kate met me at the end of our

driveway to go walking and handed back my poetry and a few chapters without comment. I stuffed them inside our mailbox to retrieve after our walk but refrained from asking her opinion out of sheer embarrassment. Halfway down the highway she said casually, "Jake asked me if you really are seventeen years old. He said the material is quite mature, perhaps too mature for a girl your age."

And from that moment on, she has treated me like a kid when it comes to my work and all else, yet she proceeds to tell "the kid" all about her marital agonies: she's seeing a psychiatrist; she's on antidepressants; she wants to meet a wonderful man and start over; they never have sex, and he's as romantic as a slug.

I've been taking out my frustrations in my journal, scribbling sometimes twelve pages a day. Half the time I can barely read my own left-handed scrawl, but it sure beats screaming out loud.

I've also been studying and going to a GED class on Monday nights. I don't have my license yet. What's the point? I know Dad won't let me drive anywhere alone. He drives me to my classes sober, but I can't concentrate on anything once I'm there because I know he's sitting outside in the car. I know what he does when he's waiting alone in the car. I pray he doesn't get too tanked by the time I come out and that we get home okay.

I've also been entering poetry contests, the kind that charge writers ten bucks for each poem that's submitted. I've received one second place and two honorable mentions. I know it's a bunch of horseshit, and they keep you baited with ego trips so you keep paying them money. But I hang them over my desk anyway.

I've also been doubling up with stomach pain that sends me to bed for three days at a time, sometimes with fever. No one knows what the problem is. I took blood tests and X-rays and even saw a naturopath. They ruled out anything life-threatening, suspected an ulcer or gastritis and recommended soft foods. All I know is that it's excruciating, and it seems I have to stop eating more and more kinds of foods to avoid an attack.

To make matters worse, The Old Bitch keeps grilling Mama about my love life, or lack of. She asks her regularly, "Emma, is she dating anyone yet? Do you think she's a lesbian?" Mama informs me that The Old Bitch says it without malice.

Mama also tells me that The Old Bitch has a woman friend who comes in from Paris once a year to stay a week or two at the Bosco estate, and more than one person has seen them holding hands while they sun-bathe together. Dad, perfectly sober, saw The Old Bitch's hand slither under her woman friend's skirt while he drove them to the city. I told Dad that he must have been hallucinating, but he insists that he saw them in the rear view mirror as clear as day, feeling each other up and smiling.

I am tired of sex. Sex, sex, sex. On the TV, on the radio, and in those books that Jackie Collins seems to churn out like potato chips. I'm sick of nosy people inquiring about who I'm not having sex with, why I'm not dating and going out and making an ass out of myself by getting laid and drunk, not necessarily in that order.

Had I been raised Catholic, I think I would have become a nun. If I were a nun no one would dare ask me about sex or consider my fat ass. If I were a nun I would never worry about who will marry a misfit like me or feel strange because the mere thought of being married makes me gag. Every married person I know is miserable, including my own parents.

On bad days Mama says she wants to leave Dad and will find a way. On better days, she says she can't leave because she's known him all of her life, that he's a good man underneath it all. She also says that he's helped a lot of people and even raised a child who is not his own blood, and he's sixty-four years old and has nobody but us.

On good days, she tells me that a lot of other alcoholics are a lot worse; he's not that bad because he's never hit either one of us. He goes to work every day, supports his family, and gets me anything I might need or want for that matter.

And the horrible names he calls us, especially me, is just the booze talking.

I want to believe that, but it's really hard. It's really hard not to agree with him when he says I'm worthless. I don't think Mama knows that he says it even when he's not drunk. He says a lot of things even when he's not drunk.

When it's really quiet, I hear his words circling in my head like vultures over a dying deer. I feel like I'm bleeding slowly, invisibly. But no, he's never laid a hand on me.

Sometimes I feel guilty, because unlike Mama, I need

sustenance instead of hollow bread. Hell is Hell, and comparing one Hell against another just keeps us trapped in the fire.

I learned that Renee's step-father battled an addiction to drugs. She told me, too, that he put his hands on her a lot, when the two were alone in the house together. Her mother denies all of it and says that Renee just wants attention. I'm not sure what to believe. It makes me feel better, though, knowing that Dad doesn't put needles in his arm.

I'm reading psychology and self-help books about challenging father-daughter relationships. Maybe it will help. I'm also trying to be extra nice to Dad. Maybe he'll get sober if I don't yell back or act bitchy.

I try to talk to him about his youth, "the old days" as he calls them, but he just sits outside by the barbeque and watches the birds come to the feeder he always makes sure is full. The birds seem to interest him more than talking to me.

When Mama's home, Dad tries to get her to sit outside with him and shoot the breeze. Trouble is he's always three sheets to the wind. He drinks when he's stressed. He drinks when he's happy. He drinks when he reminisces. He drinks when the sun's out. He drinks when the neighbor's cat pees in the driveway.

And he drinks even more when the Boscos are out of town, even when he has to take both of the Bosco's cars in for routine maintenance. The last time, Mama drove one car while Dad drove the other to save some time. I rode with Mom. For a while we were having a good time, playing the radio and singing. Halfway to the Cadillac dealership and repair shop, we noticed Dad in front of us slowing down more and more, weaving over the line. My heart started to pound when he slowed down to thirty miles an hour then twenty miles an hour. "Oh, God," Mom said, pulling to the side of the road hoping he'd follow suit. We parked on the side of the highway, and thanks to whatever angels watching, Dad pulled over, too. Mom stormed out of the car. Dad was so drunk that he barely noticed her pounding on the window and yelling to roll down the window. She knew what was coming. "Tom, come on, get out of the car. Don't get sick all over The Bitch's car. Tom!" I remained in the car, almost sick myself, and I just closed my eyes knowing how it would turn out.

He puked like a geyser all over the interior, and it took them days to clean the car so no one could detect anything amiss. Mom yelled for nearly a week, and Dad managed to stay sober, but we all knew it would start all over again before the week was out.

Mama's tired of working like a dog and covering for him, and most of all, competing with the bottle. He says she's cold, and I'm nasty. Oh, and the dog growls at him.

Speaking of the bottle, Mama knows how much liquor the Boscos have in their collection. The Boscos never drink anything but an occasional glass of wine, so to keep tabs on Dad's intake, she's been secretly marking the bottle to see how much disappears over time. We know he has his own stash, but we haven't found it yet.

One of these days I will figure out the mystery of how he can go somewhere with us and become ossified drunk when we haven't seen him touch a drop. I've searched the Jeep with a fine tooth comb, but I still can't find where he hides it.

Not that it would matter. Dad is stubborn as a mule. When he's sober he says, "I'll die before I'd ever go to A.A. They're nothin' but a bunch of fags." When he's half-lit and feeling sorry for himself he sulks because we *think* he's a drunk. "I can't believe you called me a drunk in front of the kid. Thanks, a lot, Emma. Thanks a lot."

We can't do anything but stand by and pray. No matter how we plead with him to get help, no matter how many times we threaten to leave, no matter what we say or do, he has one answer: "I like to drink."

And so he does.

It's a cold sunny day, and Dad and I are on our way into Manhattan. He's sober and on official business for The Old Bitch, but we'll have some time later. Maybe we'll go to Shakespeare and Co. or that great art supply store I missed out on last time. Zabar's is definitely on the list. I have to have some of their stuffed grape leaves.

Dad's listening to talk radio and traffic reports, so I'm reading. I have photographs stuck between the pages, old shots of Mama and Dad from way back when. In one, Mama's chestnut hair cascades down her back as she sits at the piano. She's pregnant with me, happy and lit up from the inside. In another, Dad's tumble of gold hair punctuates eyes so blue that they rival a Taos sky in O'Keeffe country. He was so handsome, well-bred, a judge's son. He raised me to never eat with my hands, to walk like a lady, and to keep my voice quiet.

I don't know what happens, but life changes a person. He still never eats with his hands and bitches if I pick up a chicken drumstick, but he thinks nothing of pissing out the garage door, just far out enough to hit the grass and in the open where The Stick Lady can see him. His once chiseled face is bloated, his nose bulbous. He's red as a tomato, and his hair has muddied to light brown.

He used to call me "Daddy's little girl." Then it was "The God-damned prima donna." When I was thirteen I hated those words under his breath. Mama wrote a song for me called Prima Donna Sunshine, to turn the meaning around. I love her for it, but I doubt that even Mama with all her talent can fit his other names for me into a catchy tune.

Dad once told me he'd always love me, even if I killed somebody; he said I could tell him anything and he'd never lose faith in me. Now we barely talk at all. I'm so invisible around here that I could get a sex change, and he wouldn't notice.

Yet some things have never changed, namely, his faith in my abilities. Once, before I quit school, he came to the high school to get me taken out of volley ball. "She's an artist, for Chrissake. She's gonna break her fingers hitting that ball around," he told the principal. I was mortified.

But looking back now, I appreciate that he took my art that seriously even if he was way over the top.

Just last month he bought me a word processor, a used one to see if I like it before he invests in something better. It means the world to me, and on a practical note, I am damn glad to upgrade from the manual typewriter.

Dad's never read a page of anything I've ever written or even asked what my book is about for that matter, but brags to everyone about me. Sometimes I'd trade his blind pride for a few moments of real interest.

I don't know where my life's going. Maybe I'll teach art somewhere. I'll turn eighteen in four months. Mom and I have talked about me moving out, getting a small place of my own and teaching classes. She told me to leave this sinking ship and to make a fresh start. She said she'll somehow survive even if Dad doesn't.

We thought that maybe I could go to Tampa, near my Aunt Helen and cousin Ariel. Ariel is like a big sister to me, a writer. She's working on her Master's degree in English Lit. Sometimes we exchange letters and poems, and snippets of Langston Hughes and Shelley. She says I should keep writing because I have promising talent. Ariel and Mama keep me going.

Speaking of writing, Mama and I visited a lady in town, a friend of a friend who is well-known in the fiction genre. She read a few chapters of my manuscript, and I had hoped to get an honest but uplifting critique. I nibbled on ginger snaps and Mom perused her book shelves while the lady combed through my chapters. After twenty minutes, she took off her glasses, pursed her lips and took obvious pleasure when she said, "You have a good grasp of vocabulary, but you have a very long way to go. You write like a seventeen-year-old."

Case closed.

If I wanted to risk being contrary, I would have told her I found it humorous that Jake had thought the exact opposite. If it didn't sound lame, I would have also told her that I had a 4-H column in the local newspaper when I was eleven. I would have told her a lot of things if I wasn't just a seventeen-year-old kid.

All I could do was thank the woman and walk out wanting to burn every page, poem, and journal I had ever written and put my head in the oven, Plath-style. Mama grabbed me by the shoulders and put her finger in my face and said, "Baby, you're crazy if you believe her. You are a wonderful writer. She's jealous. Go home and write."

"Jealous? That's insane! She has seven books in print and awards all over the living room," I wailed.

A week later, we saw Carol, the friend who set up the writing critique. She stood on Main Street a little breathless. "I was going to call you. I have to tell you something." She grabbed my arm with enthusiasm. "I spoke to my friend after she read your work. You know what she said to me?"

"Yeah, that I have a long way to go."

"What? No! She said she felt like giving up after she read your stuff. She said she couldn't believe a seventeen-year-old could be that good. Way to go, Molly!"

Well, well, well. Isn't that an interesting piece of information? Mama, as usual, was right. And more and more people turn out to be mutt faces. Who knows? Maybe Neil Diamond isn't that nice behind closed doors, either.

They say the meek shall inherit the earth, but I'm not interested. Once, before I die, I want to tell someone off so bad they crap a duck.

Dad changes lanes, still lost in his own world. I'm reading Gelsey Kirkland's *Dancing on My Grave*. I turn pages feverishly hoping to read something about Mikhail Baryshnikov. I heard they were once lovers. By Kirkland's account, the angel-faced Baryshnikov isn't that nice, either. Or good in bed. Hell, I refuse to believe it. Any man with that face and who can fly like a bird without wings is no creep and can probably send any willing woman into a fit of consecutive orgasms with very little effort.

Maybe the whole world is nuts. I got a call yesterday from Lisa, the woman who married The Old Bitch's son, Rick. She doesn't know me from Adam, but apparently she's spoken to Mama at the estate when The Old Bitch isn't home. She and Rick are divorcing, and she's cracking up. She somehow got our home number and thought she'd make a crisis call to Mama. Hysterical and almost incoherent, she informed me that she was going to jump out the window with their baby in her arms. It took two hours to talk her out of it, at least for now. I swear I think I should be the one drinking around here.

We go through the Lincoln Tunnel and come into

Manhattan. Dad locks the doors with a flick of a button, and the window washers start heading for our windshield. Dad's glad that the traffic thins out right before a guy soaks the glass with his squeegee.

We cruise for a while, and taxi cabs zigzag around us like frantic bugs. We stop at a light. Dad opens his window a few inches. A creepy guy on a motorcycle next to us salivates when he sees me in the passenger seat. "You like that? You want some of that?" Dad says to the sicko.

"Hell, yeah..."

"I bet," Dad responds, raising his window. Right before it shuts, he whispers without expression, "Bastard."

I stare at Dad and wait for him to look over at me. I wait for my father to apologize for what just went on. Not for the sicko, but for his own disgusting remarks.

But it doesn't happen. Instead, he makes small talk about the parking garage at The Essex House. I can barely listen to him. I feel dirty, pissed off, and forgotten as an unfinished cigarette flicked onto the pavement.

Sixteen rows of waves, each one the color of old jade and curled like paper, surge toward the shore in erratic patterns. A hurricane is brewing. It's February which means May here in Pompano Beach, Florida.

I'd like to say that I've made a new start, that I'm teaching at the community center, living in a nice studio, and dating a poet with wild hair and a terra cotta tan. But the reality is that I've decided to not move out. I feel I cannot desert this drowning ship in the name of personal survival.

Mama, Dad, and I are actually on vacation. The Old Bitch and her husband are jetting around Europe, and the weather is too cold to do much at the estate this time of year. Mama thought that Dad would improve if he relaxed for a few days, visited his sister, and had no stress. Funny thing is that he seems happier working. He never complains about The Old Bitch, the ungodly hours, or no time off.

He's been drunk only once since we've been here, but mainly he's been sober and resentful. Sometimes we actually wish he'd have a drink or two in him to tame the nastiness that seems to infect his bloodstream. No matter how we try to be just a family on vacation, we always end up the same way; Mama and I stick together while Dad remains on the fringe, lost in his own world that he padlocks with silent indifference.

Visiting Aunt Marie was nice. We had her scrumptious homemade beef stew, fresh pink grapefruit from her backyard trees, and pleasant conversation. After Dad saw photographs of the Pope in every room of her house and avoided her unwavering interest in whether he goes to church or not, Dad pretended to still be Catholic. He also put on his best blazer, didn't swear or touch a drop of booze. Marie's calico cat Snickers and her poodle Taffy eventually got the hint that Uncle Tom didn't like animals around his feet after he scared them off with the threat of a kick behind Marie's back. I used to think he was afraid to be tripped up, with his bad leg and all, but now I just think he hates the whole damn world.

Aunt Marie gave me the surprise of my life when she handed me a diamond bangle from her jewelry box to commemorate my upcoming eighteenth birthday. She put the bracelet on my wrist, kissed my hand and told me she had the best times of her life when she wore it. I will treasure it always.

During our stay I secretly wondered what she would really think if she knew the reality of her dear brother's life and what a stinking hypocrite and damn good actor he is. I wondered what she would think of him calling me a "fucking worthless bitch."

I wondered what she would think of him eating in front of the TV and rambling prejudice venom. He makes Archie Bunker look like a humanitarian. I don't know how he could hate so much yet have such a soft spot for the homeless people on the bowery. He takes warm coats and clothing from his closet to give to them on his way into the city.

"I hate to see a little girl cry," he says whenever we pass a child who's upset. It's not an exaggeration to say his daughter has cried every day for the past five years, and he's been heedless. When I was little, his mantra was "Just let her bounce." I guess things haven't changed that much. I'm still bouncing.

I rake the cool sand with my fingers and think about how Mama and I are a lot like him. We're stinking hypocrites and damn good actors, too. We put on our "nothing's wrong" smiles, hate him for hating the world, and do anything but get arrested trying to hide how out of control we are. The problem is that we're sober and should know better.

Who are we fooling? All of New Blair must know the guy with the limp and the slur, the one who drives the Bosco's Cadillacs and calls everyone "his buddy." We heard through the grapevine that neighbors have heard yelling coming from our house. We've seen how some people look at Mama and me, the kind of look people have when they know even more than you think they know.

The sun drops on the horizon like a punctured balloon spilling light. A ribbon of foam at the water's edge bubbles into the fading gold. This time of day always reminds me of being a little girl when we lived in the Pocono mountains. I secretly believed the last rays of sunlight piercing the trees behind my swing set were really the outstretched arms of a goddess. She was more real to me than any God I learned about in Sunday school or in Mama's Rosicrucian books. I prayed to her and watched her slowly disappear into the gray dusk, leaving a piece of light inside my heart.

Those were the days when wonderful smells spilled from Mama's tiny kitchen with the Chinese red wallpaper; I can still taste her dark homemade bread, autumn soups, and organic apple pies with walnuts and raisins at the bottom of a cinnamon crust. I remember how we'd light a candle in crimson glass each night and say our prayers before bed. Those were the days she made up for Dad when he called me a son-of-a-bitch because I couldn't stop coughing with the croup or laughed a little too exuberantly over something that had happened in school.

I look for Dad in those memories and see a man who also swam with me at the pool, took me to the jungle gym every day after school, and sneaked packs of spongy hot pink bubble gum to me with a wink when Mama wouldn't allow it. I see the two of us driving home on country roads after our excursions with a big bottle of Genesee Cream Ale balanced between Dad's legs and his casual insistence on me taking a few sips. "Go on, it's good for ya," he'd say. I was eight years old, and despite my initial hesitation, I gave in and took a few swigs. It fizzed in my mouth like creamy, bitter seltzer and went down ice cold. I knew it wasn't right, but it made me feel close to him. We had a secret, just Dad and me.

Eventually, he showed me how to steal packs of that spongy hot pink bubble gum from the supermarket. It felt like a game when he showed me how to slip the pack into my palm and nonchalantly slip it into my jacket pocket. "But Daddy, it's wrong," I'd whisper in the beginning, and he'd answer, "Oh, screw 'em. You think they're gonna miss a few cents?" Bubblegum, cinnamon, spearmint, fruity-fruit, my small and clever hands lifted them all, sometimes two kinds at once and then back for a third if I felt bold enough. Then Mama found out about our extracurricular shopping activity, and it came to an abrupt halt. "Are you nuts, Tom? What in Hell is wrong with you?" Mama was so furious with him and disappointed in me that I got belly aches from guilt. I never did it again.

There are other memories. The sound of rustling clothes and panting breath. Dad and Suzie, thirty-five years his junior getting it on in the next room while I was coloring.

It was Easter Sunday 1977, and Mama was making us all a gourmet dinner back at home. Suzie, nineteen years old, was being treated for an eating disorder and depression at the health clinic where my parents worked. She had befriended me, and I'd spend time at her house.

After Dad and Suzie finished their rendezvous, Dad and I drove home mostly in silence and pretended to look forward to Mama's duck-al-orange. I felt like I was carrying a bomb on my back, that the slightest breeze of a single thought would set it off, and Mama, the most important person in my life, would be blown to bits.

I didn't have that responsibility on my eight-year-old back for long. Mama had known right in her gut. Not long after we walked in the door Mama burst into tears and screamed, "Thanks a lot, Tom, you son-of-a-bitch!" Dad acted dumb, but didn't put up much of a fight. The only thing I remember about the rest of that night is Mama and I eating Easter dinner alone and Mama crying at intervals and reassuring me not to worry.

But I did worry. A lot. I couldn't decide whether I hated Dad or felt sorry for him. I also felt guilty for enjoying Mama's delicious dinner.

We're at Tarpon Springs, the Greek village near the

sponge docks. It's almost nine o'clock, but we're hoping to see an open shop to go into before we head back to the motel.

We find only one, on the corner. There's a guy behind the counter with eyes as dark as Homer's wine-dark sea, and he's watching me intently. I feel the heat of his gaze on my back as I make my way through his store and listen to the sound of bouzouki pulsing from the speakers. *Oh, God.* He is beautiful with skin the color of ancient pottery and hair as black as volcanic sand.

A bust of Apollo holds my attention, but the god carved in alabaster is suddenly cold and pale. The music urges me into an ancient world. In my mind the lights dim, and my feet dance on the temple floor. "Come my Lord...my breasts offer nectar sweeter than Hebe's golden cup," I whisper as my purple silk billows with my movement.

My torrid thoughts cease with the music and my browsing, much too prolonged. I avoid the owner's beautiful eyes and take the bust of Apollo to the counter where a stout woman wearing his ring wraps it securely. I take my purchase and intend to leave without glancing back, but like a scene in a corny vaudeville skit, my feet go out from under me and I make a homerun slide right on his doorstep. I can feel my hip swelling with a bruise already, but luckily, Apollo survived the fall. My handsome object of desire comes over in a hurry, half concerned, half entertained. He laughs like Zeus and offers his hand to help me up. His smile is dazzling, and his laugh lines are just deep enough to drive me crazy. "Are you alright,

Miss?"

"Yeah, just stupid," I answer, laughing off the throbbing pain.

"No, no, not stupid. Very pretty. Not stupid." His eyes tango soulfully with mine as warm salt wind blows in from off the docks. I notice the name tag on his white shirt and a small gold cross around his neck catching the light. If he was not married, if my parents were not waiting for me, if I wasn't a frigging nun, I'd throw myself down on the floor with the Gods watching, run my tongue over every inch of his delicious soul and leave nothing but the bones.

We say our goodbyes, and I step out onto the vacant sidewalk where I meet up with Mama. Dad left a few minutes ago to get the rental car. I'm shaking from embarrassment and maybe the stain of his eyes. "What happened?" Mama asks. I tell her my shoe got caught. She gives me a knowing smile. "What's his name?"

I protest and laugh at the same time answering, "Nick."

Goodnight, Nick. Thanks for making me feel...beautiful.

4

Hannah, a friend of The Old Bitch, is staying at the Bosco guest cabin. She was a successful writer in her day, and now she is battling cancer. Mama's been instructed to care for her, bring her meals, and make her as comfortable as possible before she goes back to the city for her treatments. Mama told her that I'm a writer, and Hannah offered to read some of my work.

I am a little wary of this whole thing as I walk up the steps to the cabin. I'm also nervous about meeting a woman with cancer. Cancer makes me think about dying and when Mama had it.

Mama wore thick bandages under a special bra to soak up the bleeding and washed the bathroom down with bleach every morning after she changed the staph-infected gauze. She waited a long time to get help, too long. Dad was in total denial and acted as if Mama had a hangnail. After her mastectomy, Dad, upon hearing that her tumor was the size of a grapefruit, asked, "Oh? It was cancer?" His words were monotone, disinterested, and unforgivable. But not too surprising.

That year before Mama's mastectomy, Dad was screwing around behind her back with her best friend. I saw them at the end of our driveway kissing like two oversexed teenagers, his hands groping her breasts while I thought of Mama's breast being ravaged from the inside out. They were both oblivious pigs.

By the grace of God or whatever else to which we attribute miracles, the cancer was slow-growing and had not gone into Mama's lymphatic system; she made a full recovery.

I push the memories out of my mind as I rest my eyes on Hannah in the dim bedroom. The air smells peculiar-the scent of something medicinal mixed with cedar from the log cabin. "Hello, my Dear. You must be Molly," she says. Her face broadens into a smile that looks like it takes a lot of effort. She is thin and looks like a pale fledgling bird, but her eyes are warm and beautiful. She motions for me to sit down on her bed.

"Thank you so much, Hannah, for reading some of my book. It means a lot."

"Well, you have a lot of talent, Molly. I don't think you will have a problem getting published. Just stick with it and make it a way of life. Write, no matter what happens. Don't have any excuses." My eyes well up; my words falter. She takes my hand. "Molly, you are very good."

"Thank you."

"And you're mother is right, you are a beautiful and sweet girl. Stay just as you are." She touches my cheek. Her smile is like a lantern in the dusky room. I feel like I've known her for a long time. "Well, as you can see, I won't be going anywhere any time soon, so I have time to kill. I've been listening to your mother's songs. Another great talent. I know now where you get it from. I just wish I knew someone in the music business so we can get this stuff out there. It's a shame she's had such bad luck."

"Yes, she's wonderful." I smile and silently think to myself that the worst of her bad luck was falling in love with the wrong man. Hannah goes on to talk about small things, the summer blooms and how beautiful our small town is this season.

"Come and visit me again, Molly, won't you?" she asks. She's breathless by now and wincing from pain. I know she needs rest, and I ask her if she needs anything before I leave. She shakes her head "no" before she closes her eyes to sleep.

I clutch my writing folders and cut through the Bosco's rose garden. Hannah's right, this year's blooms are exceptional, whispering delicate pinks and boasting a shade of sunlit fuchsia so intense that it makes me squint. I inhale the sweetness.

I sit down on a bench in the gazebo and realize that just maybe, there's a life for me somewhere. I also wonder what my eight-grade English teacher would say, the one who had once accused me of plagiarism after I turned in an assignment. I say a prayer that I will someday make all the naysayers gasp and that Hannah somehow gets well. I am grateful she visited my life if only for a few minutes.

It's Mr. B's ninetieth birthday celebration. We are at the Park Lane Hotel in Manhattan, and by the looks of things, it's the swankiest party in town right now. The Old Bitch thought of everything including two hundred guests, lobster tails, champagne, a Big Band orchestra, a caricaturist, and a privately published biography chronicling the sometimes amazing life of her self-made husband.

Mary the housekeeper sits next to us with her self-obsessed daughter, Amy. "Well, thank you, aren't you sweet!" Amy drawls as someone asks her about her aspirations in the fashion industry. Mousy brunette, small-town pretty and five feet tall and knock-kneed, she insists on walking around like Miss Universe. I remember her from high school and how she'd giggle and wiggle for the boys as if on cue. They called her a Siamese cat because of her slightly crossed right eye. "Gag me with a spoon," Renee and I would whisper behind her as we walked to Social Studies.

"I've just completed another portfolio, head shots and the like," she informs the poor soul who is now held hostage as she goes into detail. Before I regress to high school lingo and broadcast "Gag me with a spoon" into a megaphone, I feel a tap on my shoulder.

I look up and see Rob Bosco dressed in bone white and a black tie. "Would the lady like to dance?" he asks, smiling and taking a bow like he did the first time we had met on Christmas Eve a couple years back.

"Oh, Rob, I don't think so. I can't dance to save my life."

"Oh, come on, my toes are tough," he reassures me and bends down to kiss my mother on the cheek. Mama pokes my arm and says, "Oh, go and dance." I roll my eyes, put down my napkin and take Rob's hand onto the dance floor.

"So what have you been up to?" he asks, pulling me closer to him as I look down to make sure my feet aren't nailing his toes already.

"Um, writing a book," I say.

"A book? How ambitious."

"I don't know about that... I think ambitious would be going to India and living in an ashram." I smile. "By the way, have you been back?"

"Oh, no, no you don't. We have plenty of time to talk about me. I want to hear about this book you're writing." He leads me into waltz steps and picks up the pace once I get the hang of it. Well, kinda.

"It's about the creative soul."

"Go on. I like it already." He smiles, and I realize he has beautiful teeth, not like mine that are slightly concave with an overbite.

"In short, it's about a man, a songwriter, married to someone who doesn't understand the emotional landscape of an artist and the need to create."

"That's deep. Where'd you get your inspiration?"

"Observation," I say and leave it at that. "Artists don't have it easy."

"No, they don't. Now let me ask you something."

"Sure."

"Why did you choose your main character to be male?" He asks as he spins me around. I step on his toes and apologize in gushes. "Oh, don't worry about that. Just answer my question," he says, smiling again with such charm I feel my face flush.

"Well..." I think for an answer but cannot come up with one. I shrug my shoulders and laugh.

"I think it's so interesting that you didn't write in the voice of a woman because you are a woman. I admire that."

"Why?"

"It takes a lot of courage to step into the shoes of the opposite sex. And not many people want to venture into thinking beyond their own gender when in reality, the soul is androgynous. Our finest essence, each of us, is composed of both male and female energies." The song comes to a close, and Rob adds, "Come on, let's talk."

We go into the sitting area next to the ballroom. A caricaturist makes animated sweeps with his felt-tip pens; people line up for their turn while a little girl sits motionless in the ornate chair in front of him.

"Is this philosophy part of your spiritual studies with your guru?" I ask.

"The guru is only a representative of God-potential. The rest is up to us."

"What else have you learned?" I cross my legs and listen intently.

"That everyone we meet, everything we see, everything manifested in this physical world, is love. Love is energy. You know, it's common to think that when we fall in love with someone that we love the person, but it is really the spark of God ignited in us. If we see personal love as it really is, we can be in love with all of humanity." Rob trails off, his blue eyes faceted with emotion. "I'm sorry. It's hard to stop me once I get going."

"No, don't apologize. I love this stuff. When I was a young girl my parents took me to many places—churches, ashrams, you name it. We visited Baba Muktunanda."

"Baba's my guru!" Rob exclaims, breaking into yet another warm smile.

"What a coincidence," I answer, a little surprised.

"Molly, there are no coincidences, only synchronicities." Rob's smile lingers, and he closes his eyes briefly, savoring thoughts he decides to keep to himself.

"Hey, will you be coming to visit this summer as always?"

"You bet, and then I go back to India in September. I look forward to seeing you. I'll bring some books for you if you'd like."

"I would. Thanks." He puts his arm around me affectionately, part big-brother, part something else. I like the something-else.

"Hey, up for another dance?" He asks with enthusiasm.

"Only if your toes are," I answer with a laugh as we head back to the dance floor. On the way, I notice Mama and Dad having a good time. Next thing I notice is Dad focusing the camera on us. Rob stops to pose with me gallantly. I smile, thankful for my father's sobriety tonight. And Rob's friendship.

All Hell has broken loose since The Old Bitch found out about Mr. B's affair with his fifty-something personal assistant. The Boscos had Mama and Dad in their will, but after The Old Bitch found out that they knew about Mr. B's affair and didn't tell her, she promised to cut them out altogether.

"How dare you, you rotten son-of-a-bitch! You old bastard!" she screams at Mr. Bosco. "Do you know who I could have married? I should be treated like a queen, a queen, you filthy animal! For all that money you gave her, I hope she got down on her knees and blew you like a pro! How dare you humiliate me like this!" And on and on she goes, Mama says, all through the morning hours on the days when Mr. B is home. The Bosco estate is like a film set, and the Boscos are doing their own action scenes when The Old Bitch punctuates her screaming monologues when she throws ice water in Mr. B's face, runs after him and kicks his shins, and pulls his hair until she has fistfuls. Mama finds white tufts on their bedroom rug every morning, and she fears for the old man's safety. Mr. B has told Mama not to worry, that he is fine. He may be fine, but he sure doesn't act remorseful. He remains silent through the eruptions, continuing to read the newspaper or watch the birds bicker at the feeders outside the windows. I think that drives The Old Bitch craziest. He just lets her run out of gas. In other words, he just lets her bounce.

She continues to go to her psychic, and I continue to type the readings which now span two and a half hours. The guy tells The Old Bitch that Mr. B and his mistress were together in another life and they did away with her to be together. This sends her into near-homicidal rage. The Old Bitch is proud of punishing her husband and tells Mama every morbid detail of her abuse.

If Mr. B coughs in the middle of the night, she shoves her feet into his back and pushes him off the bed and won't allow him to get back in. Sometimes he remains on the floor for hours because he can't get up without his walking cane which is too far out of reach.

I told Mama I am ready to call the authorities on her, but Mama said that Mr. B doesn't want that and to stay out of it. Perhaps the old man's a masochist, and he married the right person. Her cruelty is nothing new, but now more than ever, The Old Bitch believes that she has earned the right to be a viper. Her compassion for poor Hannah doesn't make sense.

Another friend of The Old Bitch called recently because he felt depressed, and she told him to go kill himself.

He did.

They found the man's pill-saturated body a few days later.

And last week, the Old Bitch heard that her seamstress' husband fell off a roof and nearly died. "Emma, you just made my day," she said to Mama after she delivered the news.

"Why?" Mama asked in disbelief.

"Because I know I am not the only one suffering," she answered and then laid into the old man again and stomped in one spot like Rumpelstiltskin.

She is also more eccentric than ever. "Tom, there's an animal in the pool! Come here, quickly! Get it!" she yells to Dad during her morning swims if she sees a cricket or a mere lady bug somewhere near the water. The other day she saw deer grazing under the trees, and she asked Mama, "Emma, do you think they can get inside the house and eat us?"

Hearing about The Old Bitch's craziness makes me feel normal.

For my eighteenth birthday, Mama gives me a beautiful attaché case, burgundy leather with a brass combination lock. She says it's for my manuscript, especially when I go to see my editor. "What editor?" I ask.

"The one I called the other day."

"What? Who?" I ask, dumbfounded.

"Her name is Sarah, and she lives on Maple Lane. She's going to help you format your manuscript so you can submit it to an agent."

"But the money, Mama..."

"No worries, Baby. You're talent's worth it. And you..." she hugs me with tears in her eyes. "You keep me alive, my precious angel." I throw my arms around her. "Never mind. Don't forget to look inside," she says. I open the case and see a finely wrapped box of perfume. "I wore *Blue Grass* when I was eighteen. I think you'll love it." I hug her again and tell her that someday I will give her the world.

Dad's been on my case about getting a license and wants to teach me how to drive. Yeah, right. Does that include a shot of vodka and a six pack? I plan on going to driving school. I have more time now that I've ditched the GED classes. Dad was getting so tanked waiting for me that it wasn't worth the stress. Maybe someday.

For now I'm preparing to teach some art classes and starting a small business from the house. I figure I can teach on days and times when I know Dad will be working. I cleared it with The Old Bitch, and she said it's fine as long as I make a lot of money. I want to save up for a car so I can get to hell out of this house more often.

Kate and I still walk a few times a week, and her marriage is still on the rocks. She's still the most beautiful woman in the world, and sometimes, the most condescending.

We went to the mall for my birthday. We had lunch,

and after a day of conversation and light-hearted fun, she gave me a tiny stuffed bear with its own rocking chair. She wrapped it in paper patterned with cartooned little girls selling lemonade for five cents. Thanks, Kate. A frigging bear in a chair for all the hard work I have put into becoming a woman.

I may be eighteen, but I'm not sure what being a woman feels like. Age is just a number. I think it's sad that we're nothing but numbers until the day we die. Height, age, weight, dress size, bra size, salary, social security, address. Numbers, all of them.

I wish we could all be valued for the nobility of our dreams or for leaving a bit of kindness where we pass through. Perspective is what's precious. To me, anyway. I think polished river stones in their gray humility are more beautiful than diamonds.

"She has her whole life in front of her," people say now that I am eighteen. They ask me about college and boyfriends. I know college is not for me.

And my place, for now, is here. I resent my own choices but have no regrets. Sometimes I have so much hope that I think I'm a dreamer, like Mama. Dreams are bread for the starving soul, and I have plenty.

People look at my life from a distance and assume that I'm lazy and content with sponging off my parents. Even the Old Bitch once said that I should get a job at the supermarket instead of "writing poetry all day."

Who are we if we don't fit into black and white? What happens to people like me who trip over other people's expectations and land in the gray?

Sometimes I dream of being a storm gathering tremendous wind and speed. I dream of being a force my father and all the other bullying bastards will someday reckon with, a force they have underestimated, desecrated and dismissed with careless hands.

And I pray.

I pray the way Rob prays, for God to give me a drop so my heart can hold an ocean.

5

Mama and I are at the recording studio. Lance put down a few guitar tracks on Mama's ballad, and now we're listening to the playback. She wrote the song so many years ago that I remember being four years old and listening to her sing it while playing outside. It's one of my earliest memories.

Her voice shimmers like an angel's wing, pure and sweet yet capable of belting out a tune at Judy Garland magnitude. Some people have said that she sounds a lot like Patsy Cline. When she put down the vocal track last week, I heard nuances of Piaf and a heart broken by life but singing anyway.

Mama is at home here with a mic in her hand and mingling with people who stay up late working on a lyric and color their conversations with phrases like "and all that jazz."

I can't believe how many chances she had when she was young—managers, record companies, DJs—but it always ended the same way. The creeps wanted more than her talent, and the ones who were on the level either dropped dead or went out of business. She's had more bad luck than somebody schlepping around the Hope Diamond.

I wish I could sing, open the ocean in my veins and spill it all out. I want to scream, to be sound that splits, shatters, disturbs. I want to risk being uncorked, unhinged.

Instead, I sit here in the control room with my journal and channel the undertow through written words. Mama and Lance are wrapping things up for this session and will make another studio date when their schedules coincide around The Old Bitch.

Mama leaves happily with a tape of her new work, and she slides it into the stereo system soon as soon as we get in the car. "I'm proud of you, Mama," I say.

"I guess I'm kinda proud of myself, too." She laughs and then presses a kiss to my cheek.

"Deep breathe, hold...exhale and let the heart open like a lotus," Rob says, accentuating syllables as if each is a different gourmet flavor. I sit on the floor next to him in a meditative yoga pose as the rain plays fairy tunes on the Bosco's guest cabin tin roof. I try to focus on his imagery, but thoughts of Hannah pull at me.

She left two weeks ago intending to continue treatments in New York. Hannah once asked Mama if she would help assist her suicide so she can die with dignity. Mama had empathy and respect for the woman's request, but couldn't bring herself to be a part of it. Hannah understood and pulled my mother aside and handed her a box the day she left for New York. "The ring is for you, Emma. And the bracelet for Molly. You both have a place in my heart," she said.

We heard yesterday that Hannah had passed away by her own hand, her own way, and alone.

I look at Hannah's braided gold bracelet on my wrist. It catches the flicker of candlelight, and I vow to wear it until I get published. I will always remember her. "Don't mind me, Rob. I just can't meditate right now," I say, easing out of my pose.

"I'll go easy on you this time, but the more you think it's not the right time to do it, the more you need to do it. We'll have plenty of chances while I'm here." Rob smiles warmly and reaches for his cup of tea that is now cold.

"Tell me about India," I suggest. The gold light and his presence combined with the sound of the rain makes me glad I am here. I had not meditated as long as I had intended, but I feel a deep peace. For once I am not wondering where Dad is, how much he's had to drink, what I have to do to get food in him, or watch that he doesn't stumble with his bad leg and break a shoulder or hip.

"India is both a seductive woman and a decaying corpse. It is a place of extremes. The poverty is unspeakable."

"How do you find enlightenment being surrounded by such struggle?"

"It's the perfect training ground, to be amidst such circumstances and learn how to purify your responses to them," Rob says, relaxing on the floor against the chocolate-brown leather sofa. In this light his bronze hair looks like a weave of soft golden wool. I ponder what pastels I would use to achieve its color and texture. "But that doesn't mean I am always successful. I thought I was prepared for the level of extremes, but nothing prepares you. I know that it's changed my thoughts about a lot of things."

"Like what?"

"There is such waste in this world. When I prepare food at the ashram, I make it a meditation. I try to remember that the least, the very minute, offers the greatest abundance, in all things."

"I agree, totally. By the way, what do you usually prepare?"

"Vegetarian dishes, baked goods. I lay out the spices as if they are paints and group them by flavor, intensity, and color."

"That's beautiful," I say, smiling. "By the way, thank you for those sinful truffles."

"My specialty," Rob says with a wink. A warm wink, the kind of wink that flips my belly like a sudden drop in an elevator. "Now, Miss Molly, tell me how your book is coming along." He props up his arm on one knee and holds my eyes with steady interest.

"Actually, I have a lady who is helping me get it in perfect manuscript format—better sentence structure, margins and all that stuff. She's taught me so much."

"What page are you on?"

"Two hundred seventy-five."

"What character feeds your soul?" he asks, catching me off guard. I think for a moment, taking a sip of cold tea.

"Each one."

"Good answer. Though, it's not like having a favorite kid or anything." We both chuckle.

"Thank you," I say in a low voice.

"For what?"

"Asking about the book and for listening. Talking about what really matters. So many people go through life talking about nonsense."

"You are so right," Rob agrees and shakes his head "Hey, I hope it's okay with your parents that we hang out like this," he adds.

"Mama thinks it's great. As for Dad, he's oblivious."

"He won't go after me with a shot gun or anything, right? I mean, his daughter is very beautiful," Rob says, raising his eyes to look at me from under his thin brows. I drop my gaze.

"Thanks, Rob," I whisper, acting a little awkward, the way someone might act when they receive an unexpected gift.

"No need to thank me. It's the truth," Rob says with conviction. He brushes my hand slightly with his thumb, a whisper against my skin. "Always know I will be a gentleman."

"That's not written in stone, is it?" I ask, testing the waters. I shock even myself with the innuendo.

"Not unless you want it to be," Rob responds with a bit of a chuckle and shifts position. Now I think I've embarrassed him. We avoid each other's eyes as Rob pours more tea into our cups and the rain comes down in sheets against the windows.

The sound on the tin roof is percussive, and Rob picks out a beat with imaginary drum sticks. I laugh, and without warning, he takes my hands again and kisses them three times in staccato to not lose the beat. "I'm glad I'm getting to know you, Molly."

"Me, too, Rob." Without further conversation, we listen to the rain with our hands resting in each other's. We close our eyes and with effortless beauty, I feel my heart open like a lotus.

Scarlet berries drip from the rowan trees, and the meadows and roadsides hum with conversations of chattering crickets. It is apple time here, my favorite time in our corner of the world. Golden Delicious, crispy McIntosh, purple Winesap, sour Granny Smith—colors ranging from bright green to deep burgundy. Local cider, better than wine, goes into my apple-walnut cake, even my beef stew.

We've been living here for five years, yet we haven't picked apples at the nearby farms. Every year I hope Mama has energy and time off. Every year I hope Dad will be sober long enough. I'm eighteen years old, and I still long for a chance at a Brady Bunch family life. What a crock.

Rob stayed for two weeks. He cooked me exotic rice dishes stained with saffron and spiced with cardamom. He showed me his advanced yoga poses and read my poetry aloud with beautiful eloquence. He taught me how to eat with chopsticks. He gave me a sexy wink and kissed me goodbye on the cheek before he left with Dad to go to the airport.

He also unknowingly threw open the curtains in the dark rooms of my life, however briefly. He won't be back to New Jersey until next summer. I will miss him.

I've been filling the gap by writing, taking driving lessons, and working with Sarah, my editor. Sarah tips the scale at three hundred pounds or more and lives in a lovely house with her very skinny common-law husband. She's rough, gruff, to the point, and has given me wonderful advice. She marks my pages with blue and red colored pencils and keeps my participles from dangling.

She has also stuck her nose where it doesn't belong. "Take Brian out of the book!" she insisted over the phone recently.

"Sarah, I can't take Brian out of the book. He's critical to the storyline," I explained.

"I hate him!" she informed me with passionate intensity I never dreamed she'd be capable of.

"I appreciate your advice, Sarah, but Brian's staying in the book." End of subject.

Two days later, she handed me freshly-typed chapters and pulled me aside with a low voice. "I'm sorry if I overreacted the other day. That damn Brian of yours reminds me of my ex-husband," she confessed, trying not to spit. Her face flushed like a boiled lobster when she said the words *ex-husband*. "And besides, I'm curious about something."

"What?"

"How many times have you made passionate, soulful love?"

"Not many," I said, secretly wondering how she mustered up the audacity to ask me such a question.

"I thought so."

"Why?"

"Your love scenes are something *I've* never experienced."

"That's too bad," I said, refusing to believe that lovemaking is mechanical and unremarkable as reading a plumbing manual.

Or learning how to drive for that matter.

My instructor Alan is a nutcase with pop-marked skin, thick glasses, and a tendency to scream at me with four-letter words to get his point across. Last week I was out with him in the student driver car, and I was going seventy-five miles per hour on Interstate 80. "You're not going fast enough! You're driving like a God-damn old lady! Come on, dammit, step on the fucking gas!" he yelled.

"I'm already going fifteen miles over the speed limit!" I yelled back.

"If the rest of the cars are going eighty, then you go eighty to keep up with the flow of traffic!"

"Where did you learn how to drive?" I asked him.

"Look, if you want to drive, I'm here to teach you!"

I learned how to parallel park on a one way street with seven cars lined up behind me while I got the hang of it. I expressed my preference to let the cars pass so I could park in peace, and Alan screamed on top of his lungs, "No way! You park under pressure, and you better get it right."

And I did. I got it in one shot. I looked over at Alan; he shook his head as if the ninny girl did something right for a change.

I see how a lot of men look at women, at me. I've seen that look on my own father. Sometimes I secretly hope that I will turn out to be a lesbian. I think of wonderful men like Rob and wonder if the demeaning streak is there somewhere under the surface waiting for the right circumstances to bring it out.

It's Saturday, and I will be teaching my third children's class. I have five kids signed up, and Billy, the seven-year-old, tests my patience. With his fiery red hair and personality to match, the kid is rude, hyper as a live wire, and could probably turn Mr. Rogers into a raving maniac.

The mothers seem very pleased with my four hour curriculum of art instruction, nature studies and organic lunches. Dad works during those hours, so the coast is clear in case of any unexpected booze binges. He doesn't ask me anything about my classes except, "Did the little nippers come?" which he says with a sober smile when he comes home. It's the same smile he gave me when I was little, and he was still my best friend.

I'm surprised Dad doesn't inspect the house to see if anyone dropped any food. I remember being a kid and eating watermelon outside with Mama because Dad forbade us to eat it in the house. He was sober back then but still a pain-in-the-ass control freak. God forbid a seed or drop of sticky sweetness escaped the plate. When he wasn't home, Mama and I would have fun by eating watermelon and deliberately making a mess, laughing until we got belly aches.

I wish I could go back and be a real kid who is allowed to make a mess once in a while, slide down a staircase railing, or express glee by jumping up and down with little-girl squeals. "Act like a lady," Dad would say. Or the obnoxious, "Stifle yourself and be quiet," line of shit.

These are the ridiculous things I think about when I'm around my students, when their faces light up like supernovas, and they scream with delight when something makes them happy. When I see fathers who don't care if their kids accidentally spill their bags of trail mix on the way out to the car or slam the car door a little too loudly.

Prima Donna Sunshine

A part of me lives vicariously when I hear about a little girl sleep-over.

Observing my students makes me remember things I had forgotten about, things I had gotten used to. Dad didn't want my mother or me having friends or visitors. Kids from school who tried to befriend me or kind neighbors who brought us holiday sweets were quickly escorted out of our house or thrown off our property. Mama would yell at Dad until we all almost went deaf, but it never changed anything.

I saw a little girl at the farmer's market this morning. She had chocolate-brown hair and freckles, and she giggled as she ran through the sprinklers. Her spirit was clean and beautiful like newly-turned soil. I wondered what seeds would blow into her life.

How infinite, how vulnerable we all begin at the mercy of the winds.

6

It's the same every morning. I am awakened by the sound of Dad's dry heaves. He's better once he gets coffee in him, but his hands shake like someone with Parkinson's disease until he replenishes his stash of booze. The liquor store opens at eight-thirty in the morning, and he gets there ten minutes earlier and waits until they let him in. I watch him drive down the road in front of our house, pause at the stop sign, and then make a slow left-hand turn into the strip mall behind the trees. I watch his routine from my bedroom window and imagine that every morning he vows not to go across the street to the liquor store the same way I vow not to cry when I see him do it. But we do anyway. It's probably the only thing we have left in common.

Winter's coming in with an early bite. Everything seems on pause and on the verge of something ominous. Even

Schnapps has been uneasy, howling in his sleep like a hound from the Baskervilles. The horrific sound wakes us from sleep and makes the hair on our arms stand on end. I've read in Celtic folklore that the cry of the banshee sounds a lot like that and visits families to warn them of impending death.

Even freakier, Dad has been moaning in his sleep like he's wrestling with demons. Mom shakes him awake, and he tells her he's having the same dream again. He dreams he's stumbling in the dark, trudging up a long flight of stairs and trying to find the light switch. I ain't Freud, but that dream sure tells me a lot.

I've had nightmares of my own lately. I dream that all my teeth are falling or that I'm drowning in dark snake-infested water. Last night I dreamt of Zane, my biological father. I saw his face in a blood-red moon rising over the mountains.

Despite the past, Mama has been talking about contacting Zane. She thinks I have a right to connect with my roots, and perhaps, after all these years, Zane could offer a sense of family that I crave. I told her I would think about it, but I already know it is exactly what I want.

I also know that after I die I want my ashes to be scattered in the ocean. I requested some literature from The Neptune Society. It gave Mama the creeps. She asked me why I'm thinking about dying. I told her there's nothing wrong with thinking about dying, and dying might come sooner than later. "You're going to have a long life, Molly. Don't be so morose," she advises.

She's my sweet mother, and I know her job is to try to keep my thoughts on what other eighteen year olds might think about. But I'm not like most eighteen year olds. I'm not into the music of Madonna, Bon Jovi, or Debbie Gibson. I listen to Beethoven, Richard Wagner, and my old love, Neil Diamond. I read Poe and Rimbaud. I wear Bohemian vintage skirts and Gypsy earrings, shun acid-wash jeans and never step into clothing stores at the mall. While hair trends say to punk, mousse, and chop, I wave and wear my hair long, halfway down to my waist like a Pre-Raphaelite painting. Mama knows I've always been like her, a person who goes against the grain. But she worries about my dark moods, especially since she found out that Renee tried to kill herself two months ago.

Apparently, Renee moved near Princeton to go to school. She's cut herself off from her entire family, including her aunt Patty who is praying that she finds her way.

Patty and I hit it off and are becoming fast friends. She lives half a mile down the road, and we go to flea markets and thrift stores for vintage finds. She has boyish cropped hair and has the look and peaceful energy of a Buddhist nun. She can repair a furnace, wear flowers in her hair, and talk mechanics and spiritual philosophy with the same amount of passion. She takes in homeless cats and dogs and anyone who might have lost their way.

Patty also has a lot of experience with alcoholic families; she herself grew up inside a whiskey bottle and knew poverty well. She goes to Adult Children of

Alcoholics or ACOA meetings. It hasn't taken her long to figure out Dad's problem. She humors him, and Dad, behind her back, refers to her as "the fag" because she's got the butch vibe going. To his chagrin, Patty is hopelessly straight.

I talked to her once about my fears of being gay, and she said, "So what? Who cares?" and went on to tell me how, after husband number three, she decided to become a lesbian.

"And?" I asked, anxious to hear how her experiment turned out.

"Shit, Molly, I tried. I really, really tried," Patty said and let out a smoky laugh between cigarette hits. "I even had ménage trios."

"And how was *that*?"

"Stupid." We both laughed. "Then husband number four came along. He was the best and worth waiting for, God rest his soul." She winked. "And besides, lesbianism isn't a choice. Are you really attracted to women or are you just rebelling against men?"

"Sometimes I think both. That's why I'm confused," I confessed. "Mainly, I love older men and beautiful women. But I think it would be easier to love women."

"You're wrong, Sweet Pea. Love is love, and love can be hard." She paused to take another drag on her cigarette and then said, "Wait! I didn't ask you an important question."

"What's that?"

"Are you okay in a woman's body? You don't want to be

a guy or anything, right?"

"Oh my God, I want to get away from men, not become one!" She laughed her butt off after I said that and decided, "Honey bun, just take life as it comes. By the way, have you talked to your Mom about any of this?"

"I've hinted at it. She thinks I'm going through a phase. Thanks for taking me seriously."

"From what you tell me about your Mom, I think she'd want you to be happy, no matter what brand of love you're cut out for."

"I hope so, Patty," I said.

She's asked me to go to a few ACOA meetings with her and even investigate Al-anon. I told her maybe someday, but not now. The last thing I want to do is to sit around with a bunch of strangers and talk about Dad. Patty thinks I am making a huge mistake, but I am sick to death of all of it.

Snow falls in whispered constancy this morning. Schnapps is curled in sleep on the gray round-back chair as I look through Mama's memory box. She gave me her souvenirs from her years with Zane so I can see what kind of love they shared before the turmoil. I pore over volumes of Sufi and Japanese love poetry, letters held together with turquoise ribbon, and elaborate nineteen sixties greeting cards. There is even a page from a calendar torn out with September 21st circled in red. It was the day I was conceived, the day they met at Zane's New York City apartment, and Zane gave Mama three red roses—one for her, one for him, and one for the baby they wanted to make.

Mama told me that she had met Zane when she and Dad were nothing but roommates. She was all set to have a new life with Zane, her soul mate, or so she thought. Until the day he hit her and dragged her on the floor by her hair.

She was terrified of him and wanted to protect the life of her unborn baby, so she did everything to keep him cool, even pretending she was still going to make a life with him in New York once I came into the world. But she secretly knew that she would never marry a violent man, no matter how she loved him, especially when there was a child on the way.

Mama went back to Dad who was then a teetotaler and compared to Zane, uncomplicated as humans come. He was sterile from an ulcerative bladder infection he suffered when he was eighteen, so he welcomed me and saw a chance at fatherhood as a miracle. Mom finally broke it off with Zane, but he stayed in the peripheral of our lives, a predator to my mother when Dad was at work and I was at school.

I take a deep breath and wonder what he will think of me all these years later. I have not seen him since I was a child when I knew him simply as Uncle Zane, a friend of the family. I remember his impeccably pressed white shirts and brown bow ties, his quirky love for pickles, and his engaging stories about the night sky. I especially remember the time Dad, Mama, Zane, and I had vacationed at Cape May for five days. I was ten, and we all gorged on sea food, sat on the beach at midnight and ate fat pancake breakfasts. "Uncle Zane" taught me about shells, how to look for sea glass, and bought me a faceted Cape May Diamond necklace.

I also remember him screaming violently at Mama while I hid out in another room until the storm passed, hours later. I also remember him telling my mother that my childhood stammer wasn't normal and to meet with people he knew who had a mentally challenged kid.

I wonder if he's mellowed or if he's even interested in knowing his daughter. I also wonder if he could live up to the romantic fantasy I've had of him all of these years since I stumbled on the truth at fourteen when I had been looking in my mother's closet for a box of greeting cards and came across a manila envelope. Inside were photographs of Uncle Zane, probably in his early thirties. His cheek line and his nose looked just like mine.

I didn't have the courage to ask Mama outright if Zane was my real father, so I wrote her a letter. She came into my bedroom with tears in her eyes. "I was waiting for the right time to tell you, but I wasn't sure you could handle it. Are you okay?"

I took that as a "yes" to my question.

"Yeah, just shocked," I said. "It explains a lot, namely why Dad and I are like fire and water." I paused, overcome by tears. "Does Dad know?"

"Yes. But he's always seen you as his. I think it would

break his heart if he knew that you know..."

"It probably would," I whispered.

We never told Dad that I knew about Zane, and I walked around for a long time with a smile on my face. At fourteen, I thought it was romantic that I was a 1969 love child, and my real father was a crazy Van Gogh. I told my best friend Debbie by scribbling it in a note during math class. Her blue eyes widened to cartoon roundness when she read it, and I told a few more friends just to get the same dramatic response.

I close Mama's box of memories. In a way I feel that my longing to know Zane is a betrayal to Dad, and I don't even know why I give a damn. Sometimes when Dad's really drunk it takes every ounce of strength not to tell him that I'm glad he's not my natural father. I imagine it to be the perfect revenge for years of having my heart rupture from the weight of his words.

The Delaware River moves like a cold snake between its icy banks. It brings back memories of being ten years old when I spent a weekend with Zane. He lived in Pennsylvania, right across from the river. We swam in its amber waters every day that weekend, and Zane tried to teach me how to dive off the rocks. But I was a chicken in a one-piece, flag-patterned bathing suit. The red and white stripes curved over my pot belly, and the longer I stayed in the water the more the Navy blue crotch collected with water and sagged under my butt like a saturated diaper.

I replay that weekend in my mind as we cross the Lackawaxen Bridge. It was the weekend Zane taught me how to do a still life in charcoal, sign my artwork with an artist's signature, and how to not be afraid of the water. Two out of the three were a success. For two nights in a row, I had dreamt of seeing a skeleton at the bottom of the river, a heap of bones wearing my bathing suit. That didn't help matters when I got back in the river.

It was also the same weekend I saw ghosts in that old Victorian house where Zane and Lorraine, his second wife, lived. I spent a night seeing three women in nineteenth century dresses swish past my bed. I hid under the covers until dawn, but I still couldn't escape the sound of their tapping heels across the hardwood floor. I prayed for them to go away as much as I prayed for my bladder to hold out until dawn. There was no way I was going to get up in that dark room and go through an even darker hallway to the bathroom, not with three crazy spooks on the loose.

Zane was an atheist and didn't believe in anything but art and the human spirit, so he lectured me for a long time about how there is a plausible explanation for everything mysterious. Lorraine winked at me from across the room as if to tell me that he was the one who was out of the loop. She later took me aside and told me that she too had ghostly encounters in that house.

Despite their vividness, those times seem incredibly distant. A lot has changed. I come back here a woman; Lorraine passed away five years ago; Zane lives in another house and is remarried. He sounds gentler. "I'll take as much or as little as you can give me," he told Mama on the phone last week.

Dad, surprisingly, is cool with the whole thing even though he thinks we're all having some sort of demented Hippie-inspired reunion with Uncle Zane. He's sober and a little cocky as he rings Zane's doorbell. I don't know what to expect and hide my trembling hands inside my coat pockets.

Before I can think about it another moment, the door swings open. Zane looks the same, just older and with a lot less hair. He's wearing brown slacks and a white shirt with the same gold cufflinks I remember from long ago. He glances toward me with a wistful smile and invites us in.

He hugs Mama first, a long hug with tears and quiet excitement. Mama breaks up the seriousness by slapping him on the arm and saying, "You look good, you old son-of-a-bitch!" Everyone laughs, and Zane shakes hands with Dad and gives him a hug. I'm on pins and needles knowing I'm next.

"Look at you, all grown up. Molly, you look so much like your mother," he says, embracing me gently. He pulls away, and I expect the same sentimental warmth he has in his eyes when he looks at Mama, even Dad for that matter. But it's not there when he looks at me. I figure Zane's just in shock.

It's a blur of conversation, introductions to his new wife Linda, and a tour of the house. Linda is a petite woman with a salt and pepper Twenties bob and an abundance of energy. She reminds me of a tiny twister as she talks about her passion for cooking, gardening, and breeding German Short-Hair Pointers; they have two, Ivan the Terrible and Angel, each aptly named.

Every once in a while, Zane puts his arm around me, but I still feel a distance I cannot quite put my finger on.

Perhaps he doesn't know what to make of me. I was a flat-chested, klutzy eleven-year-old in grass-strained denim the last time he saw me. Maybe it's my anti-twentieth century ensemble of Victorian boots, long black skirt, Danskin leotard, and replica Roman coin jewelry. Or maybe I'm not pretty as he had hoped. Maybe he's just not that interested in this whole father-daughter bonding idea.

I try to shrug off my uneasiness and watch him speak with enthusiasm. I see so much of myself in him. We both have dark hair, rosy English skin, and round, heavy-lidded Russian eyes with a flicker of melancholy in the green. We definitely have the same nose, but I think it looks a helluva lot better on him.

I linger in his studio as everyone heads to the dining room for lunch. His canvases are more beautiful than I could have remembered. Windswept sand dunes against flame-blue skies, portraits and nudes, and early spring landscapes fill his studio. There is a pastel portrait of Mama in a gold antique frame propped up on an easel. Her skin is flawless as fresh cream, and her burnished chestnut hair hides the naked fullness of her breasts. It gives me goose bumps.

He keeps his supplies neatly placed, stored, and categorized. There isn't a hint of abandon anywhere. I was secretly hoping for some evidence of madness, the kind you'd expect in the studio of a passionate, sometimes-crazy artist. His drafting table overlooks a large picture window with a view of gnarled fruit trees and a dark pond fringed with ice in the distance. I imagine what it must look like in the summer. I hope to spend some time here, in this place, and in this room; I hope to have a kindred spirit.

I glance over at Mama's portrait once more. Zane's passion for her is evident in every blended stroke of pastel. I don't quite know *that* Mama, the one whose heart has not yet shattered against life. I am happy Zane painted her in the spring of their love so long ago. I am happy to be their daughter.

It's a bitterly cold night, and Dad is standing alongside our car with a police officer. He is testing Dad's faculties to see how drunk he is. We left Zane and Linda's house a half hour ago. He did it again, tanked up on booze right under our noses without us knowing it. It must have been when he went out to warm up the car. Mom is sure he's done it this time, and he will lose his license.

The lights from the police car are blinding. Our faces are flashing crimson, and my heart's pounding. The officer has already shone his flashlight into each window and asked to look in the trunk for any open bottles of booze. He didn't find any. One part of me prays that Dad somehow gets out of this. The other part prays he will lose his license

Prima Donna Sunshine

because it might sober him up. Something has to.

"Mr. Dorman, please repeat the alphabet from A-Z and speak slowly," The officer says. Dad is pale as a ghost and gets through the alphabet with hesitance. The second test comes. "Mr. Dorman, please walk in a straight line ahead of me." Dad walks in a straight line, as straight as he can with his bad leg. "Mr. Dorman, how much have you had to drink this evening?"

"Only a couple. I'm fine, Officer," Dad says, sounding surprisingly sober.

"I was behind you for five miles, and you crossed the yellow line ten times, Sir."

"I didn't realize it, Officer. It is dark on these roads."

"Yes it is, Sir, but there is alcohol on your breath. I should take you in for a breathalyzer test, but since you did not fail these tests and your record is spotless, I will let you go this time." The officer proceeds to look in the open window. "Mrs. Dorman, may I see your license?" he asks. Mama takes it out of her wallet and hands it to him. After a brief inspection the officer says, "Mrs. Dorman, will you please drive the rest of the way home?"

"Of course," she says and gets out of the car.

"Mr. Dorman, your wife will drive the rest of the way home. Please get into the passenger seat."

"Yes, Officer. Thank you, Officer," Dad says as he gets into the car like a beaten dog with his tail between his legs. His hands are shaking, and I can tell his mouth is dry as cotton.

Son-of-a-bitch. Dad never fails to ruin a good day. I can

almost set my watch to him screwing it up every time we laugh too much. I am beginning to distrust happiness.

7

Mama and I come home from grocery shopping and find Dad like a beetle on his back in the kitchen. It didn't take him long to get plastered while we were gone. "Oh, thang God yur back," he slurs with his eyes half rolled up in his head. "I tripped with this fuckin' leg uf mine. Where the fuck did ya go?"

"To the store, Tom. What in Hell are you doing, Tom?" Mama responds. She's mad as a wet hen. Schnapps is barking his head off by now.

"Nether mind that shit, jus get me up. And shut that fuckin' dog up before I belt him."

"What if we leave you there until you sober up?" I ask and then turn to Mama. "I think we should leave his sorry ass right where it is."

"We can't, Molly," she says, grabbing his hand to help him up.

"Get the kid," he says. I hesitate a few feet away. "Hey lard ass, come here and help yur mother."

"If you call me lard ass one more time, I'm not helping anybody get you off that floor," I spit back.

"Emma, get that worthless kid over here."

"What'd you say, Tom? Did you call my kid worthless? I don't think you'd be alive if it weren't for that kid holding up this goddamned house and putting up with your shit," Mama says, threatening to kick him in the ass.

"Emma, please be nice, God dammit. Why do ya always hafta be a nasty son-of-a-bitch?"

"You never call The Old Bitch nasty. That woman makes our lives Hell, and you never say a word."

"She's a doll, leever alone," Dad answers. "She dussin mean anything." I crack up laughing until I realize that he is actually serious.

"You got it for The Old Bitch, don't ya, Tom?"

"Go to Hell, Emma."

"Okay, you're staying right there," Mama decides.

We bring the groceries in from the car and just walk around him as if he isn't there. I like turning the tables for a change. I really rub it in by making as much noise as possible. I slam cabinet doors, crumple paper bags, and stack cans like bricks. I put dishes away and clank them just short of shattering. If I were Greek I would break plates for a week. "Emma! Emma! I'm gonna die down here. Gemme up, fur chrissake! Molly, you worthless lil lard ass. Somebody help me!" he rants. Each time the rant gets louder. "Get that lil cunt over here," he says to Mama when he catches her eye on the way into the pantry.

"Say that one more time, you drunken son-of-a-bitch, and your good leg won't be worth anything," Mama shoots back.

"Oh, God, gemme up. I can't take anymore. Emma!" He starts crying. He looks like a one hundred ninety-five-pound blubbering baby. He cries, yells, rants, and mumbles to himself under his breath. Some new profanity even makes its way into his already-vast vocabulary.

Mama and I look at each other. "I can't take much more. He's pathetic," Mama says. I agree, and we each grab one of his arms and try to pull him up with all of our strength. He's dead weight. We almost fall backwards in the process, but we finally get him up on the fourth attempt.

"It's about time," he concludes then stumbles into the bedroom like a crab on roller skates. Mama stays behind him so he won't go down again.

"If you break a hip and get laid up, I'll kill ya," Mama warns him.

"Ah, shut tha fuck up," he says as he collapses on the bed, halfway off. "Emma, take these shoes off, will ya?"

"Oh, God!" I wail with exasperation as Mama pulls his shoes off and throws them down on the floor. "Mama, you're crazy!"

"He's pathetic, Molly. I feel sorry for him," she says, staring at him staring at the ceiling.

Prima Donna Sunshine

"How about feeling sorry for us for a change?" I yell and slam the pantry door. Schnapps runs for cover in my bedroom.

A strange silence fills the house. I go to Schnapps and find him curled up in a quivering ball. "It's okay, Baby Love," I whisper. "I'm sorry we're all nuts." I can hear Mama crying in the kitchen. I'm too angry to cry.

Mama comes in and puts her arms around me. "I want you to get out of here, Molly. You can't stick around for me. It's too late for us, but not too late for you," she says.

"I love you so much, Mama." I hug her.

"That's what I'm afraid of," she whispers.

This morning I woke to find a note in the kitchen from Dad. It's written in his usual haphazard handwriting that looks like ancient hieroglyphs:

Baby, I am so proud of you for getting your license. I knew you could do it! You've never made me happier.

While I appreciate his pride for accomplishing something so ordinary, I'm also pissed off at the fact that he's never expressed such enthusiasm for anything else I've done like writing a book, teaching classes and having a small business out of the house, or putting up with his crap all these years.

We're in another ungodly heat wave. I can see mirages shimmering in the distance as I walk over to the Bosco estate. I ascend the steep driveway and glance to my left at the neighbor's house halfway hidden by cypress trees. I have heard that the guy is an artist with four hyperactive kids and that his work is in demand around the world, though I do not know what he paints exactly. I always try to get a glimpse of his studio.

The scent of the cedar trees is pungent from the humid weather, and wood thrushes sing in the thickets. I jog uphill to get there a little faster because Rob is in town, just back from an ashram in upstate New York.

The guest cottage door swings open, and Rob greets me with a megawatt smile. "Wow," he says, staring at me.

"What?" I ask, hoping he can't see how stressed I've been.

"You look...all grown-up." He continues to smile.

"Rob, it's only been a year. But I am nineteen, not exactly a baby." I laugh, and he lets me in.

"Nineteen looks good on you, Ms. Molly." He gives me a hug. We linger. He smells like sandalwood and patchouli. He pulls away slightly and then brushes his mouth gently over mine. A million thoughts go through my brain like crazed bats.

Oh no, this isn't the way to become a lesbian!

I need a friend more than I need a lover.

Shit, Dad better not find out.

Hey, I could always run off with Rob and live in an ashram.

Damn, I think I'm in trouble.

While I was growing up, the trees were where I brought

my heart's unuttered longings. The big old white pine behind our house in Pennsylvania had a bed of fallen needles a foot and a half thick. That old tree witnessed my blubbering fits, heard my prayers, and served as a hiding spot when I had a temporary case of boldness and ran away for two hours. I remember lying down on the russet softness and inhaling the sweet, pungent scent while I whispered prayers in the wind. A few times Dad had to use a comb soaked in turpentine to get wads of resin out of my hair. It was more stubborn than bubble gum and had to be cut out when all else failed.

I haven't had a sacred spot like that until now. I have reserved a corner in my bedroom for a prayer altar. Zane, here for his fourth visit, takes one look at it and advises, "Don't have any sacred cows, Molly. Religion is the opium of the people."

"We need sacred cows, something to get out of bed for," I argue. He doesn't like it that I wear a tiny silver cross around my neck or have an image of Mary Magdalene on my prayer altar. But the picture of Baba Muktunanda that Rob gave me from India really gets him riled up. "And don't be fooled. There are no holy men, only charlatans. Some are more convincing than others."

"Zane, it's just a space in the house I go to when I'm feeling stressed. Don't get all worked up," I say, keeping my spiritual passions to myself.

"What's the fascination with Magdalene?" he asks, looking at me with curiosity that borders on suspicion.

"I am drawn to her legends, even the possibility that

she might have been a priestess in a matriarchal order rather than a prostitute," I say, leaving out the fact that I also pray to her in hopes of washing away the filth I feel in myself these days.

"Don't tell me you're a feminist," he says with a smirk that would be cute if not for the obvious distaste in his eyes.

"Maybe," I say in hopes of challenging him.

"It would be a shame, Honey Child. Don't lose your femininity."

"Did you ever read women's history? Even the Church condoned wife beating."

"Let's not get into a debate, Gloria Steinem," he says, attempting to change the subject. "And speaking of femininity, take your hair out of that tight pony tail. It makes you look like a dyke."

"A dyke? Since when is a pony tail a sign of lesbianism?" I ask, secretly terrified that he can read my innermost struggles.

"Oh, come on, it's a beautiful day out there. Let's go somewhere," he says. I let it go with reluctance, and we decide to head for the lake.

Bluegrass is almost knee-high and thick with clover. Cows graze in the distance, and the hills look like sun-dappled patchwork quilts. Zane puts his arm around me and squeezes me affectionately, almost with apology for his unrestrained opinions. "Tell me how important art is to you," he inquires.

"Well, I see writing as my calling, and art I guess, is my

love."

"What about passion?"

"Aren't love and passion the same?"

"Hell no! Passion is the fuel that keeps you doing what you love even when it becomes a love-hate relationship. True for art and marriage." He winks. "You sure have given me a new lease on life, Honey Child."

"Me, too. I look forward to our Tuesdays. More than you know..." I trail off.

"How bad is it with Tom, Molly? Your mother filled me in for the most part."

"I never know what to expect. I've learned to take one hour at a time because things change fast. Our lives revolve around him. I don't know if it will ever end."

"I battled my own demons, went to A.A. I became a sponsor, and let me tell you that it's never too late. I've seen drunks with only weeks to live come off the street and turn their lives around."

"That gives me hope."

"He just hasn't hit bottom yet. You can't make it easy for him."

"It's more complicated than that. What happens to him happens to us. The house goes with the job. We have no money. It's scary. And underneath it all, I know Mama won't leave."

"Know I am always here. I've missed a lot, but I'm here now." We hug. I feel safe for the first time in years. "Just keep art in your life, beyond teaching. Have it for yourself, too. Someday it will be your lifeline."

"Experience talking?"

"At times it's been the only thing between me and suicide," he confesses. I read the unelaborated pain in the deep furrows between his brows. I am secretly glad to hear that he's thought of checking out, too. It makes me feel less guilty. "Hey, it's a beautiful day. Why are we being so serious?" he asks, putting on his favorite goofy grin. He makes me laugh as each of his animations morphs into the next. He could have been a comedian. He bends down to pick up a stone and throws it across the lake. It skips three times and then sinks. We skip rocks like two kids. Occasionally we startle frogs or turtles near the shore line.

"Hey, I have something for you," he says when we get back in his truck. "I'm glad I didn't forget to give this to you before I head home." He reaches into the back seat and wrestles with his usual pile of necessities including a coffee-filled stainless steel thermos, notebooks and sketchbooks, and a tape recorder for any spur-of-the-moment epiphanies. "Ah, here it is." Zane settles in his seat and hands me a three-inch-thick book of full-color Impressionist works. He shrugs off my elation. "Just make sure the inspiration leads to some new paintings," he says.

Before he leaves, I hand him my unfinished manuscript at three hundred and twenty-one pages. "Wow," he says with a smile. "Are you finished with it?"

"Nope. In fact, I've haven't worked on it in a while. I just can't concentrate on it with everything going on right now."

"I look forward to reading it, Molly." He hugs me and

then puts on his hat. He checks to see if he's forgotten anything and rummages in his pockets for his car keys. He hands me a fifty dollar bill, and I protest, but he insists that I take it.

"Thank you, Zane. Really," I say.

"See you next week. And I want to taste that mean chili of yours. I know my chili, so it better be good," he warns with a playful smile on his way out the door.

After he leaves, I look in the flyleaf of the art book and read his inscription:

To the lovechild of my universe. With love from beyond the stars.

It's good to have a comrade, someone who greets me with a pocket full of plans. There is something that sets him apart from everyone else I have ever met. Last week he snapped off a sprig of pink blossoms from the tree in front of our house and stuck it in his hat while he recited *Desiderata*. We bounced around town and ate ice cream cones in frenzy before they melted in the heat.

I can see why my mother fell deeply in love with him so long ago. I hope someday to feel that for someone. Rob is wonderful, and I may even let him have my virginity. But I don't think I could fall in love with him. I look at Kate during our walks, and I think I could fall in love with a woman. I don't know what to make of myself. Sometimes trying to figure it all out seems like too much. Of all the puzzles in my life, I am the most difficult. It frustrates me to think that selves aren't puzzles, and we just can't throw the pieces up in the air and say to hell with it.

8

"My heart belongs to my spiritual path, and I know your heart belongs to your work, Molly," Rob said to me this morning as we sat on a picnic table overlooking the lake. "I will be leaving in a couple of days, and I will be in India for two years, perhaps forever. It's where my soul is calling me." He paused to smile. "As a kindred spirit I will miss you, but as a man, I know I will regret not making love to you." We kissed, and the wind blew my hair around his face. Skin, muscle and bone seemed to liquefy, and we were no longer solid, separate beings.

"You'd be the first," I whispered.

"And I'd be honored," he said with a smile I pressed between the pages of my memory so I would never forget it.

Making love with Rob seems the most natural thing to

do. The past three weeks have been filled with walks by the lake, hikes, and meditations when he wasn't in the city. I lied through my teeth to Dad about my whereabouts, and Rob did the same with The Old Bitch. If she ever caught wind of this, she'd be planning the wedding of the century.

We're now at the Bosco's guest cabin, in the small white bedroom with the pale window shutters. I stand naked in front of him, patterned in violet Paisley of late afternoon shadows. My heart's pounding like surf. "I'm not perfect," I apologize, thinking of a million flaws magnified by the sunlight.

"You are a daughter of God, therefore perfect," he whispers, tracing his words over my breasts that Mother Nature never quite evened out. "And you just happen to be beautiful, a morning rose." The incense we lit a little while ago is burning slowly; its gray-blue ribbon of smoke curls its way through a shaft of sunlight and up toward the ceiling.

My self-consciousness loses its grip as I lose myself in the slow rhythm of his hands on my body. Birdsong drifts in from the open windows as he tells me that the vital energy of the universe is called Shakti or feminine power and that the male is powerless without this life-giving force. You make me feel like a goddess," I say, my words muffled by his arms. The color of his skin reminds me of caramel, and I brush my tongue along the line of his strong shoulder. His aquamarine eyes are beautiful in this light, and I can almost see his ancient soul shimmer in their depths. My nervous hands unbutton his shirt and pause at the zipper of his khaki pants. "It's only me, Molly. There is nothing to prove or be afraid of," he assures me as he helps me help him out of his clothes. We laugh all the way to the bed. "It's my first time, too," he says, adding, "My first time, with you..." We laugh and meld into a tangled knot of limbs and warm hands, bellies pressed together in synchronized breath. It feels like meditation but with less effort. He swells against me as we move in serpentine time. "Don't worry, I took care of it," he whispers and slips on a rubber. Against the heartbeat of sunlight, he is inside me, a slow silken blade opening pomegranate. My juices spill, and I silently wait for the pain to subside into pleasure. I run my hands through his bronze hair as he moves on top of me. I want him to fill the bottomless pit of my life; I want him to look me in the eyes and pour his soul into mine until I drown in forgetfulness.

But he seems lost in the dance instead of me, in an ecstasy beyond what my body could possibly provide. Painfully, beautifully, Rob is inside me but somehow outside of me in a world all of his own. He is, as Rumi says, drunk on God, and I am simply the doorway.

But I am content. There is little pleasure on my part, only surrender to a new self. A part of me feels like a new butterfly fresh from the chrysalis—wet, changed, vulnerable—more vulnerable than I ever thought I could be.

The setting sun leaves its gold goodbye on the window sill before splashing the bedroom floor with light.

Everything seems suspended in time. Our bodies are still pulsing when Rob circles me in his arms and surrounds me like a cocoon. This small white-washed room holds the vanilla afterthought of champa incense, and the sheets smell like Rob's earth and my ocean.

Dusk comes in on gray wings, and Rob's whisper in my ear startles my reverie. "I don't want you to go," he says.

"I don't want to go," I answer, shuddering to think about going home. "I just want to call my mother to tell her where I am."

"Sure." He hands me the phone by the bed, and I dial the main house.

"Bosco residence, Emma speaking."

"Mama, it's me. I'm with Rob at the cabin."

"Is everything all right, Baby?" she asks.

"Yeah, fine. I want to hang out here a little while longer."

"Just don't get pregnant," she whispers into the phone. Oh my God. Mothers know everything. "And don't worry about your old man. I'll be going home soon and will handle everything. I'll mums the word," she assures me.

"Thanks, Mama. I love you."

"I love you, too, Baby. Be happy." I hang up, and Rob puts the phone back on the receiver. I nestle back into his arms as day fades; twilight kindles into sapphire.

Breath rising, we merge again. Scarlet of passion and blue of soul. Violet unity.

Rob and I both know there are no strings between us, and we would dissolve back into our separate lives. I didn't expect to feel the ground go out beneath me when I watched Rob in the Bosco's Cadillac disappear down the driveway.

I can still feel the dampness of his kiss on my mouth and my cheeks as I make my way through the acres of cedar and maple on the Bosco's property. The emptiness in me that his body had filled is vacant again. I kneel beneath an umbrella of leaves and rake the earth with my fingers.

I feel hollow as if the wind is blowing through my core. Tears come from the gut, so deep I wonder if there's an end. Not because I am in love with Rob. I won't miss him the way a lover misses another.

It's a simple and undeniable realization; no matter what happens, what I do or where I go, in the end I am still stuck with Molly Dorman.

She's a four-door heap of metal, a Toyota Corolla with a lot of miles to her name, but she's mine. I named her Blue Eyes. She was a Bosco company car a year short of heading to the junk yard, and I bought it for a song. Her engine has a lot more life in it and should hold me over until I can upgrade.

It feels good to get to hell out of this house more often. I had some extra money left over after I paid the car insurance, and I did something unthinkable: I went shopping at a few department stores. I almost checked my temperature this morning when I woke up with a yen for some trendy clothes. Today was the first day in a long time that I allowed myself to do something frivolous; I loved it.

I bound into the house with my packages and find Dad sitting at the table with a couple of drinks in him. He doesn't say "hello" but launches into a verbal trip down memory lane. It takes me off guard because aside from telling me how much he had hated his mother, he never talks about his past. "Your mother and I had a lot of good times," he says, staring out the window. November's pale cheek blurs the glass as ravens pick at the brown grass on the front lawn. "The world was better then. You would have liked it."

"I know I would have," I answer and sit down across from him. He's sober enough to be totally coherent. He's actually talking to me.

"We used to order seafood take-out and rent a boat. We'd eat in the marshes and watch the sun go down. Brooklyn was great."

"Do you miss it?"

"Yeah, the way things were back then." I go to the kitchen to get a glass of water. "And your mother was a knock-out."

"You bet she was a knock-out. I saw those pictures. She still is, you know," I say.

"Oh, I know." He shakes his head in agreement. He continues to stare out the window. I sip water and study him. He looks vulnerable, something in the way he's sitting in the chair. He looks handsome in his light pink shirt and chocolate brown slacks. His tiger eye pinky ring reflects the light coming in from the window. For the first time in a long time I remember how much I love him. "Man, she had a pair of legs," he says with emphasis. "She was gorgeous, a piece of ass." I wince at the reference and quell the criticism burning on my tongue.

"Mama could have been a superstar."

"She was better lookin' than you'll ever be."

"What?"

"Fucking right," he answers, his eyes still glued to the passing cars outside the window.

"You're right, Dad. I can't hold a candle to her," I agree flatly. The last thing I want to do is let him know that he just kicked the breath right out of me.

I feel paralyzed but manage to pick up my shopping bags and head for my room. He doesn't seem to notice and continues the conversation with himself. Barely audible, he mumbles, "Fucking right. Worthless son-of-a-bitch."

I heave the shopping bags on the floor and close the door. It's out of character for me to not analyze what just went down. I don't even approximate how many drinks are in his system or ponder the source of his cruelty. I don't resent my beautiful Mama for being something I never could.

I just cry until there's nothing left.

"Wow, you sure can cook, Linda," I say to Zane's wife

who has just replenished a platter of baked acorn squash and placed it on their big oak table. My mouth is sticky with honey, and Zane makes me laugh by pointing it out.

"Come on, Woman, come over here and eat with us. You slaved all day in the kitchen," he says to Linda, making exaggerated motions with his large hands.

"I'll eat later, as I always do," she answers, lighting another cigarette and taking another sip from her can of beer. She shoots Zane a dirty look and tries to hide the fact that she hates it when I come to stay for the weekend.

Deep down I think she knows Zane still loves Mama. He told me he does. Despite warm camaraderie between Linda and me in the garden or in the kitchen, I know that my presence reminds her of Mama and Zane's once-in-a-lifetime love affair.

Ivan the Terrible is still sulking by the window after two squirrels taunted him through the glass an hour ago, and Angel is sleeping at Zane's feet under the table. She's his favorite. She has a silken coat and an adorable talent for smiling and showing both rows of teeth like a goofy human. "So what do you think? Are you up to drawing your old man tomorrow?" Zane asks me after he finishes his third helping of acorn squash. I pause in a moment of lightheartedness and secretly wonder how he doesn't blow up with gas. I've never seen a person eat as much as him in a single sitting.

"Sure," I say, putting my napkin down with emphasized commitment.

"I want to see how you work with a live model. An

artist proves his worth by how he works live, not by photographs. Bah humbug to photographs," he grumbles.

"You have worked from photos, Zane," I remind him.

"Yes, only coupled with the live subject. A photograph can never capture the nuances of living, breathing subjects."

"You're right."

"You will find that I am a tough teacher."

"That's okay. I'm on board."

"Yeah? You'll need a tough hide around me," he says with a look of challenge glinting in his eyes.

"I'm no ninny, Zane Davis. And a good artist," I remind him.

"And you can be even a better artist."

"Yes, I can."

"Ah, Honeychild, it's so good when you're here. You bring life back to these old bones again," Zane says, grabbing my hand across the table and smiling.

"Don't sound so damn old."

"Young people always say that until they get old," he grumbles again, this time with a wink.

"You do act like an old fart," Linda chimes in from her spot by the fridge.

"Ah, be quiet, Mrs. Davis. I've earned the title of Old Fart."

I laugh as they bicker back and forth, and Angel picks her head up from under the table. She smiles at Zane, probably in hopes of a few scraps. "Come here, my precious girl," Zane says to the dog, and as if on cue, she jumps into his lap with surprising swiftness. "Oh, that's my Angel, my lovey. Such a good girl." Angel slaps his face with her tongue, and Zane is like a big kid as he plays with her.

"Now *that's* the real Mrs. Davis," Linda remarks, trying to hold back a smile. I laugh as I help Linda clear the table. Zane and Angel's love fest progresses to a wrestling match on the living room floor.

After the dishes are done, I decide to turn in early and go upstairs to Zane's studio for the night. It's a small oasis equipped with a twin bed, kitchenette and a private bathroom. I kick off my shoes and take a deep breath. Despite occasional tension with Linda and Zane's unpredictable philosophical rants, it's good to be here. It's good to be with a father who asks me about my life and my feelings and calls me "Queen of the Nile" with affection.

I still have to avoid topics such as religion and feminism, but I can let my spirit roam in possibility for the most part. Zane and I can talk for hours about philosophy, literature, beauty, and art; my mind never goes hungry here.

There are times when Zane intimates that he wants me to call him "Dad", but I just can't go there. Dad will always be Dad. Despite everything, he's earned that. He's raised me from the beginning.

It pisses me off, though, to know that Dad remains sober as a judge when I'm gone. I'm happy for Mama, of course, that she gets a break from the insanity. But I know that the day I return home he'll go right back to his booze routine.

Zane asked me if I'd consider moving in with him and Linda and understood when I declined his generous offer. He knows I wouldn't leave Mama, and I'd lose my home business. But I appreciate that he cares that much.

I lean back on the bed with a pile of books from Zane's vast collection—Gurdjieff, Nietzsche, Omar Kyam. I breathe in the blessed calm. Somewhere outside, an owl's shrill call pierces the December darkness, and sleep takes me even before I complete a single page.

9

I am sitting on our blue hard-ass sofa listening to Mama belt out the song "Summertime." Joni, a lady who is auditioning Mama for her Fifties vocal quartet, plays our piano with gusto, but I barely notice her. All I can focus on is the woman in front of me, a woman who I no longer see as just my mother. I have heard her sing all my life, but today she rivals household names. The hair on my arm stands up. God damn. Why is she working for The Old Bitch and putting up with Dad? What went wrong?

Mama concludes the song, cracks a joke, and bursts into her exuberant smile. Joni turns around slowly. She looks like she's got a bad case of whiplash. Damn, I'd sell my soul to give somebody whiplash by singing a song.

Joni clears her throat and mumbles something. I think it's about arrangements she's working on. "Emma, I like your voice, but it's too dominant," Joni says. "We're all about harmonies, and no one stands out."

"I understand," Mama says.

"Oh, good," Joni says and then scans our book shelves, and it lightens the tension. "Oh, you have Edgar Cayce in your bookcase!" she remarks with enthusiasm.

"A like-mind?" Mama asks her.

"Cayce, Seth, Corrine Helene- spiritualism, mysticism. Emma, you're right up my alley! How'd you get into all of this stuff?"

"When Tom and I lived in New York years ago. We went to metaphysical lectures. It was great. Not like the Hollywood New Age trends now."

"Yes, I know what you mean," Joni says.

Mama and Joni bond over books, and I am happy to see them hit it off with shared interests. I curl up on the sofa with a legal pad and try to finish my outline for the next chapter in my book. But it's no use.

It's been months since I've been able to finish a page, and I simply don't give a rat's ass about it anymore. I feel guilty as if the manuscript is a neglected child. I've put nearly four years of my life into this book. It would be a shame to abandon it when I'm so close to The End.

Then I think about nature, its power of destruction seems to equal its power of creation, and without what Rob called Kali, there would be nothing new. "The reaper and the mother are one in the same," he told me last year. It's a good thing to think about when I feel like a quitter.

Maybe I'm just too depressed to conjure anything

these days. Dad lost his license this past February. The brakes failed on his way home from the city. He nosed the car ahead of him as he tried to slow down at a stop sign. He had only a couple beers when he stopped for lunch on the way home, but it was just enough for the cops to throw the book at him.

The only reason The Old Bitch didn't fire him was the fact that faulty brakes, rather than Dad's imbibing, caused the accident.

Since Dad won't be driving again until September, the Boscos hired another driver for their needs. Dad's been responsible for maintenance of the estate. The great thing about it all is that he's been sober as a judge because he can't get his booze anymore. He's stopped shaking and heaving in the mornings, and now he only binges on orange juice.

The down side is that Mama and I have been driving his nasty hide around everywhere. *Everywhere* does not include the liquor store, and he sees us as his jailors.

The fact is, he's a pain in my ass. He's gotten more controlling than ever and has say over everything except my bowel movements.

Having him in the passenger seat is even worse. "Put your blinker on," he squawks a quarter of a mile before I have to make a turn. "Slow down, you're gonna get me killed!" he yells if I go over forty miles an hour. "Go easy on the brakes," he orders if a squirrel jets out in front of the tires. "Turn off that God-damned noise," he grumbles if I have the radio set to the classical station. "I don't want that fucking thing!" he snaps when I remind him to put on his seat belt. "Please, Molly, just one beer...I promise I'll have only one. Just take me to the liquor store," he pleads almost tearfully. "You're cruel," he decides when I keep going right past the strip mall.

"Get out!" I screamed yesterday, pulling over to the side of the road. It was supposed to be a leisurely summer drive on the back roads past the horse farms, but Dad made sure he made it miserable every mile. I couldn't take it anymore. "Dad, get outta my car, right now!" He looked at me with disbelief.

"Don't scream at me," he whined as he put his hands over his ears like a little kid.

"I swear if you don't shut up about my driving and everything else, I'm leaving you right here. You can walk home."

"Alright, Warden, I'll be good. I promise." He shook his head and tried to hide a smile as I pulled back onto the road. "You take after your mother."

"You'd make Jesus lose his mind."

"Never mind that, look at the horsies," he said, pointing to the thoroughbreds nibbling in the pastures.

"Dad, in case you've forgotten, I just turned twenty."

"Aw, come on, look at the horsies." I looked over at him instead and just shook my head. "You'll always be my little girl."

"I'm not a baby."

"Remember when you'd sit on my lap, and I'd feed you breakfast?"

"Oh, God, here we go. Yeah, Dad, I remember."

"You'd point to what you wanted and say 'beansies' or 'eggies'."

"And then you'd say, 'Are you really, weally Daddy's little girl?'"

"You were so cute," Dad said with nostalgia. "Until you got a big mouth like your mother," he added matter-of-factly.

Yes, I have a big mouth. Some days it's the only thing that saves me from doing something unthinkable.

Unthinkable. How many "unthinkable" things can I come up with in a day? I ask myself as Joni and Mama share a pot of peppermint tea in the kitchen and talk about everything they have in common. It's good to hear Mama laugh. She's been doing that a lot these past few months since Dad's been sober.

Now back to *unthinkable*. Take Blue Eyes cross-country; hook up with a woman lover somewhere in New Mexico and a get a tattoo along the way. That's one scenario I like to entertain when I'm feeling brave. *Unthinkable*. Move out to California, hang out with poets and play djembe on the beach and never look back. Unthinkable is a place I go to often.

I signed up for a women's spiritual retreat next week in the wilds of Pennsylvania. Mama thinks they will all be lesbians. I'm secretly hoping she's right.

I walk barefoot with twelve other women in single file

through marshy grass on our way to the Medicine Wheel. "Be sure that each step you take honors the earth beneath you. She is your mother," Melissa, the retreat leader says. She is a beautiful specimen of middle age with smooth skin the color of the Sahara and a voice melodic as water over stones.

Dee, one of the participants, almost steps on a snake in the murky water between her toes. She shrieks like a rabbit in the jaws of a coyote, and I don't blame her one bit. "Just open your heart and send out love," Melissa says. "I have walked in barefoot meditation through the Everglades countless times. I have been surrounded by cottonmouths and have never come to harm. It's all about bringing your being into harmony with your surroundings."

I try to focus on serenity as the image of water moccasins sticks in my head. Some of the women start singing a Goddess hymn. I join in. *Ancient Mother I hear you calling...Ancient Mother I hear your song...Ancient Mother I hear your laughter... Ancient Mother I taste your tears.*

It's exquisite here. The retreat house is perched on the shores of a lake; we wake each morning to polished silver as far as the eye can see. We are surrounded by woods, wetlands, meadows, and fields. Aline cooks us gorgeous vegetarian fare and thanks the spirits of the harvest as she prepares our meals. We meditate on Goddess archetypes, pray for the Earth's healing, and try to connect to our deepest selves. Sorry to say, there is not a single lesbian on the premises but all good and wonderful souls. Far from even the nearest town and the usual chatter of my civilized brain, I have never felt more like myself.

We ascend a stark incline and finally reach the Medicine Wheel. Each direction is marked with a weathered pole streaming with colors that represent one of the four elements. An inner circle is constructed with meticulously-placed stones and crystals.

Melissa lights white sage in an abalone dish and instructs us to walk through its pungent smoke. "Synchronicity, Sisters, is the greatest gift when we have eyes to recognize it," she says as a red tail hawk circles overhead.

She leads us into meditation, and my chest feels heavy. Perhaps it's the burning sage or the morning's journaling exercise into our past wounds. I feel off-kilter. "Breathe deeply and surrender yourself to anything that is weighing on your heart," she whispers. It doesn't take long for a few women to sigh or surrender to quiet tears. I feel angry, but I doubt that Melissa wants us to vent our anger on sacred ground. I breathe deeply, keep my eyes closed, but I still want to scream.

It's the same thing over and over again, a memory I keep in a cage so it can't get out and claw at me. It's been testing its boundaries since we got into digging up the past.

I don't like to go over any old roads, I remind myself when the image bites at my heels or gets into my cells. *Maybe I'm wrong.*

It's in my body more than my mind; it flashes like heat

lightning inside my bones. I shift in my place within the circle to avoid giving in to the scream stuck in my throat: *Don't touch me!*

I am little again. Hands where they shouldn't be. Then ten years old. The year I wore those green pull-on pants. The same year my behind grew out of little girl flatness, and my breasts started to bud through my t-shirts. Dad hugging me a little too long. I want to squirm away, but he won't let me go. "Come on, let me rub the cute little ass," he says in his cutesy voice as his hands slip down my pants. He rubs my behind until I start to hate it and yank away. "All right, all right," he resigns and pulls my pants straight, so straight they reach up to my chest and jab me in the crotch. He gives me a kiss on the cheek and it's forgotten, no harm done.

And another time, "Come on, show me the cute little ass. Pull down your pants so I can see the little, round ass," he says until I flash him my bare butt with embarrassment.

And that year when we moved to New Blair. I was thirteen years old. Dad walking into the bathroom unannounced after I step out of the shower with a towel halfway on. Soft terry, white with yellow stripes, the same towel I take to the beach. "I'm not lookin' at anything," he says with exasperation when I cling to the towel and shoo him out like a fly. No apology. Total innocence on his face as he asks me if we need anything at the store. Dad walking into my room as I'm getting dressed and my jeans are on halfway. More than once. More than twice. No apology. Total innocence on his face. All is forgotten, no harm done.

A full moon hovers above the trees. It's our last night here, and Melissa is offering us readings with her Tarot deck. I never really had a serious or accurate experience with card readers, but I decide to go ahead with it just for fun. She asks me to shuffle the cards then cut the deck while I ask a silent question that I'd like answered. I really want to know where in Hell my life is going.

Melissa spreads the cards out in front of me and pauses for a long time. "There is a lot of turmoil in your spread," she begins with an air of caution. "I see a house burning down, but not literally. They are showing me chaos on the home front."

"You've got that right," I say, already intrigued and wanting to hear more despite a chill of apprehension that runs down my spine.

"You must take care of yourself. It will be a critical time the next couple of years or so." Melissa touches the second row of cards. "You are so creative and have so much potential, but don't expect much fruition for a while. It will seem as if everything you touch is a locked gate. You will feel obstructed." She narrows her eyes as if she's peering through an invisible key hole. "And death...a father figure, an accident. In the summer, when there are a lot of flowers in bloom. The spirits are imploring me to prepare you and your mother." I swallow hard. No one here knows of our struggles with Dad's addiction. My hands start shaking. "I don't mean to upset you, but I must tell you what I'm getting."

"No. Please go on." I silently wonder whether it's Dad or Al she sees splitting the scene.

"I see locked gates stretching ahead of you. You try each one earnestly, but they are not opening." Melissa pauses. Her eyes flutter open, and her face flushes with a smile. "But you will unlock them, eventually. Most of all, true abiding love will be waiting for you." She takes my hands in hers, and she looks deeply into my eyes. "I have lived through a lot, my Dear…breast cancer, a violent ex-husband, my daughter raising a child with special needs single-handedly, and demons, more than I can count. But let me tell you, we women carry a lot on our shoulders. Some of us carry more. You are stronger than you think." My eyes well up. She shakes my hands with hopeful enthusiasm. "Love waits for you. Just get through the gates."

I thank her, and she gives me a hug.

I am still shaking a bit when we all settle into our final meditation circle. Memories of these past four days flicker with beauty despite the emotional upheavals. I will remember these ladies. Debra with her love of dance and her snippets of wisdom. Dee's beautiful hand-crafted jewelry made with copper and crystals. Aline's nourishing heart in her delicious, wholesome food. Brittany's spirited oaring on the lake as we talked about female priests in the early Church. Laurie's talent on the classical guitar. And most of all, Melissa's grace and tenacity of spirit. They all have given me sustenance for the journey ahead, wherever it leads.

Melissa's sage fumes, and pillar candles sputter their light against the breeze coming in from the open windows. The women sing and invoke the Sacred Feminine. Mary the Madonna, Diana, Kali, Bridget, Athena, and Inanna. I open my eyes, just enough to keep a soft, steady focus on the candle flame.

I notice another woman present, someone who I don't recognize. I blink to clear my vision, but the strange woman remains. She stands across from me, above Aline who is sitting on her knees. She is old, Native, with centuries engraved in her raven-dark eyes. Her long, wooly robes reach to the floor. Her gaze is so intense I can almost feel it pierce my skin. I look around at the other women, but they are unaware of her presence. "You are reaching your age of power," she says and then vanishes before I can even wonder if I'm going crazy.

I close my eyes and push out a long exhale as I realize I must have had a visitation. But what would she want with me? And what did she mean by my "age of power?" Maybe Melissa's Tarot reading left something out, something amazing. I try to hold in a smile, but I can't.

There is magic in this place. I pray I will be able to hold onto some of it after I leave. I pray Melissa's reading was wrong. I pray for everything I can think of until I have no prayers left. Proud of my lineage, I give thanks for the beauty and strength of women.

10

I have abandoned my bra, and it feels great. I don't wear anything revealing, mostly loose clothing. This July heat is even more reason not to be bound up.

I want to know which sadist invented the brassiere and string him up by his walnuts. I can't believe how some women claim to love wearing such a barbaric invention. My mother, namely; she even sleeps in one. Mama says that "the girls" will be down to my knees before I'm thirty if I don't support them, but I tell her I'll take the risk.

My bra rebellion and new philosophy of feminine freedom has morphed into other phases of my life. I used to shave if I had a mere hint of peach fuzz. Now I just let it go once in a while. I'm not talking yeti, just stubble. It's already making men snarl. This alone makes me want to keep doing it.

Patty and I went to an A.C.O.A meeting this week. Her

acquaintance was passing both our houses on his way there, so we hopped in for a ride. He sat next to me during the meeting and was a complete gentleman all night. Until he dropped me off at my house. "Shave your legs next time," he growled right before I got out of the car. I glanced down at the hem of my jeans to analyze how much he must have seen. I figured no more than half an inch of bare skin when I crossed my legs. It sure got him in an uproar.

"Don't bet on it," I answered and shut the door.

The next day Patty heard about his remark, and she said, "Honey bun, next time we'll let our armpit hair grow, and we'll braid it just for him." She made me roar with laughter.

I'm going to miss that lady when she moves to Hawaii next year. She's got her eye on a little house not far from the beach where she can forage for wild papayas and hang out with artisans who create art from shells and driftwood.

"When's the fag moving?" Dad asks. I just ignore him and decide that I have one more reason to read another book on feminism.

I've been gorging on the controversial works of Mary Daly, Judy Grahn, and Audre Lorde. Not long ago, Zane and I got into it after he said, "Back in the frontier days, women were real women. They worked harder than men and lifted cast iron pots that weighed almost as much as they did. They made sure they took care of their men and their kids. They were women with real purpose."

He's a pain in my ass, too, but he means well most of

Prima Donna Sunshine

the time. He and I sure have a blast when he comes over.

On the fourth of July, we all opted to get ice cream instead of seeing fireworks. Dad, Mama, and I all piled into his truck with our goodies and went for a spirited ride on the moonlit back roads. Zane was on one of his natural highs, cracking jokes every other second and acting out crazy scenarios as he zoomed around hairpin turns. Mama and I tried not to laugh too hard to prevent our ice cream from flipping out of the cones. "Slow down, slow down!" Dad yelled from the passenger seat as he held onto the dashboard for his life. "I don't have brakes! Where are my fuckin' brakes?" he asked in panic as his right foot repeatedly reached for a brake pedal out of chauffeur's reflex. If Mama and I didn't know for a fact that he hadn't touched a drop of booze, we would have assumed he was crocked to the gills.

"He's just nuts," Mama concluded, and then we broke up laughing again.

Some days I am convinced that both my fathers are nuts.

Last week Zane came over for a chili lunch, and he was full of questions. "Do you get enough privacy living at home?" he asked, nosing around my private life. "I hope you get enough space to have a love life," he said.

"Zane, I have no love life," I informed him.

"What do you mean? You're a twenty year old American woman. Twenty year old American women have sex lives."

"Not this one."

"Are you saying you're a virgin?" he barked.

"What if I was?"

"It's not normal to be twenty and a virgin," he informed me with obvious discontent in his knitted brows.

"Why are you so personally offended by the fact that I might be a virgin?"

"I'm not offended."

"It looks like it to me," I answer with an annoyed chuckle.

"Well, are you?"

"For God's sake..."

"When did you lose your virginity?" he said as if testing me.

"Zane!" I gasped at his audacity and laughed out of sheer embarrassment. "Last year, if you must know..."

"You are normal, right?"

"Normal?"

"You are into men, right?"

"I am quite normal, Zane Davis."

"I hope you're not one of those types who wear rose-colored glasses. Hell, if the human race waited for love there wouldn't be one."

"You're being really base right now."

"Oh, don't take me that seriously. It's good that we can talk about anything," he says, lightening his tone. "Hey, I'm starving. Where's my chili?"

And that was that.

I wonder how many gaskets he'd blow if he knew that I've been sending away for gay and lesbian newspapers. I live in the boonies without a single homosexual out of the closet, so how else can I feed my curiosity? I took on an assumed name and requested that the papers be delivered in care of our address. I'm the one who gets the mail every day, so there's no risk in being found out.

Today I received a new paper wrapped in plain brown wrapping, one from Boston. I flip through it looking for someone who looks like me. Not much luck trying to find a lipstick lesbian, but I know they're out there somewhere. Not much luck trying to find someone who feels like me, either. What do I have to do? Put an ad in one of those papers and call myself a part time lesbian? Is there such a thing?

Sometimes I like to read the pen pal section just for the hell of it. I am surprised to see a lot of women prisoners who would love a steamy letter from a woman on the outside. I feel for them and wonder why they're locked up in the first place.

No matter how I program myself to go full time, the part time lesbian in me resists promotion. Yesterday I passed some highway workers, and the guy holding the stop sign was so hot that I almost crashed into one of the orange cones. His Levis clung to a perfectly chiseled body, the kind of perfect a woman dreams about wrapping her legs around. His sunburned shoulders contrasted his white tank, and right then and there I forgot all about gay and lesbian newspapers.

My Sapphic contemplation disappears the moment the phone rings. It's Mama. Mr. Bosco collapsed, and he's on his way to the hospital. I hang up the phone with a sad tug at my heart.

The Old Bitch is probably happy. She's made Mr. Bosco's life a living hell since she found out about his indiscretion. She's probably picking out the coffin this very moment and telling the funeral director how she's been an abused wife.

A storm brews outside. Schnapps comes under the table where I'm sitting, and I give his ears a playful tug. I usually love thunderstorms, but I feel nervous today. Something in my gut tells me there are changes coming. I think back to Melissa's reading at the women's retreat and wonder if she had seen Mr. Bosco passing away. He is sort of a father figure. It's summer and everything's in bloom as she had predicted.

Lightning scars the pewter sky as I doodle on a writing pad and try to plan my next art class. The kids have been wonderful. I am toying with the idea of displaying their work somewhere publicly, perhaps next year.

Next year. I convince myself that Dad and Zane will still be here. They're not going anywhere. Zane is too ornery to croak, and Mama and I have fought too long and hard for Dad to bail out just yet.

Mr. Bosco passed away after being in the hospital for ten days for acute pneumonia. He died with seventeen Old Bitch-induced stitches in his right shin and the memory of his wife's sentimental blessing, "Rot in Hell you dirty, old bastard."

Prima Donna Sunshine

At least now The Old Bitch can't get at him. I will remember his quiet wisdom and his love for the birds that came to his feeders every morning. During his last year I noticed silent longing in his gaze when he looked out the window.

Rest in peace, Mr. Bosco. I hope your soul has flown into eternal, soft-spoken April where the birds are singing.

This summer seems endless, hot and humid as a steam bath in Hades, and Schnapps has fleas for the first time in his twelve years. Mama and I vacuum twice a day to keep up on the infestation. Sometimes we put on The Doors and vacuum at one in the morning while Dad watches the boob tube. Mama takes care of a few rooms and then I do a few more.

I'm still driving Dad around and threatening to leave him on the side of the road. My skin has been proof of the stress levels.

After weathering my teens without a pimple, my face broke out with vengeance. I tried everything without results until Patty suggested some natural supplements. When I read her list of suggestions to purchase at the health food store I asked her if she really wanted me to ward off vampires. "Just give it a shot, Honey Bun," she said.

I stuffed myself with her recommendations and am happy to report glowing skin once again. Thanks, Patty, you hedge witch.

Death seems to be lingering in the air since Mr. Bosco's passing. While driving Dad around this past week, we came across a tiny red kitten in the middle of the road. I rushed out of the car to keep him from getting hit. When I got a closer look I realized his eyes were sealed shut with puss, and he was infested with maggots. He was barely aware of my presence as I scooped him up off the road. Dad reluctantly held him while I rushed over to the animal hospital with tears streaming down my face.

Mama always told me that Dad loved cats and would even carry one or two in his shirt pockets during his twenties. He went everywhere with them. That's why it shocked me when he started cursing, "Jesus Christ, why are we wasting time going to a vet? Do you know how much they're going to charge us? Fuck this! A bullet would be cheaper." I looked at the suffering creature in his hands and screamed at Dad without remorse. "You selfish son-of-bitch! You are so sick."

Had I allowed myself to go crazier than I already am, I would have strangled my father right then and there. For the first time in my life, I truly wanted to hurt him, dig my fingers in his eyes and kick the ugliness out of him until he begged for mercy and I could say, "A bullet would be cheaper." But all I could do was keep driving so I could get the poor animal some care and pray it wasn't already too late.

But it was. They put him down swiftly and humanely as Dad waited and cursed in the car. I kept my eye on him through the window just in case he got enough nerve to take off for a drink. His rant of profanity caught the attention of a few shocked people on their way into the hospital. I went out of my way to somehow let them think I didn't know him.

The doctor charged me minimally and thanked me for trying to spare a life. I got back in the car and informed Dad of the outcome. I was too choked up with tears and anger to look at him.

I heard a moan next to me as I started the ignition, and I looked over at Dad. He was sobbing uncontrollably. "This world is so fucking cruel," he mumbled into my shoulder when I hugged him. It was the first time we had hugged since…I cannot remember.

"Sometimes so much rage comes up inside me that I wonder where the tsunami goes when I stuff it down," I say to Zane. He's sitting across from me in my room with a mug of strong black coffee.

"Like your mother and me, you are a person of strong passions. It will make you a great artist, but it can destroy you if you don't learn how to handle the fire."

"How do you handle it?" I ask, slicing a fragrant apple into slivers.

"I don't know if I *handle* anything," he confesses. "After I came back from the South Pacific, after World War Two, I had a complete nervous breakdown that lasted four years."

"What happened?"

"I couldn't function on any level. They gave me a diagnosis and sent me home. My first wife nursed me through it and paid for my art training at Hussian in Philly. Art saved my life," Zane says, taking another swig of coffee before setting the mug down on the cedar chest that is now our temporary picnic station. I swallow bites of apple and listen as he continues, "I drank, beat up the women I loved, got married and divorced more times than I'm willing to admit," he pauses. "I also put your mother through Hell."

"I think Hell is part of love, no matter how hard we try to avoid it," I comment. Zane laughs.

"This wisdom coming out of the mouth of a virgin?"

"Zane, we already discussed this," I say, looking at him with exasperation.

"Making love once doesn't count," he decides with an air of dismissal. "Speaking of making love, I saw a beautiful film last night."

"What was it?" I slice another bite of apple and dip it in peanut butter.

"I tuned in halfway and didn't catch the name of it. It was about an older person falling in love with a much younger person. The love scenes were exquisite."

"Sounds different. It's good to see the grays of love instead of black and white, stereotypical love affairs."

"Do you have any taboos, Molly?"

"Such as?"

"I don't know, anything. You name it."

"I don't have any taboos. Love is love, and as long as

you're not hurting someone with your brand of it, then to each his own. 'Love and let love' is my motto."

"What do you think about homosexuality?"

"As I said, love is love."

"What do you think about pre-marital sex?"

"I think marriage is between two people and doesn't always have to involve a legal document, so again, to each his own."

"Multiple partners versus monogamy?"

"Again, to each his own as long as other people are in compliance."

"How about incest?"

"Incest?" I feel the peanut butter lodge in the back of my throat.

"I thought you didn't have any taboos." Zane folds his arms across his chest.

"In other cultures and times, perhaps. But in this culture? No, I *don't* think so," I say, trying to act sophisticated while I feel my face burn. I hope he can't see my true reaction because he already thinks I'm an inexperienced ninny.

Zane picks up his coffee mug nervously, and it spills onto my beige rug.

"What's wrong with me? You can't take me anywhere," he says awkwardly as he tries to soak up the spill with napkins. "You make me crazy," he adds.

Uncomfortable beyond words, I tune out what he has just said and round up our plates and change the subject. "It's getting late," I say as I check the time. "I have an appointment at four. Sorry, Zane," I lie.

"No, not at all. As it is I should have left an hour ago," he says, gathering his things in organized haste. "See you again next Tuesday, Honeychild?" he asks, hugging me goodbye.

"I'll call you to confirm. I may have to drive Dad somewhere for The Old Bitch," I lie again.

"Sure thing. Love you... and don't do anything I wouldn't do," he says as he leaves, waving over his shoulder without turning around. I shut the door, straighten up, and grab my keys.

I'm out of the driveway minutes after Zane pulls onto the road. *You're a paranoid, sheltered nun*, I tell myself as I fly along the back road past the dry creek bed. I see Kate up ahead, and she waves me to pull over. "Hi," I say.

"Hey, let's go for a walk soon. I miss our talks," she says as she wipes her forehead with her hand. She is impossibly beautiful with the sun in her sage green eyes. She turns slightly to avoid the light, and her hair is the color of good brandy. I have an unexpected, sudden urge to kiss her.

"Yeah, sorry about that. I've been busy chauffeuring Dad around."

"Is he still driving you crazy?"

"Uh huh," I moan and roll my eyes.

"Jake and I are separated," she blurts.

"Damn, I'm sorry, Kate..."

"It's for the best. Anyway, I don't want to keep you. You look as if you're in a hurry."

"We'll catch up soon."

"Sounds good." She smiles and presses a graceful hand against the car door. I watch her in my rear view mirror until she's a crimson dot vanishing into the horizon.

I pump up Stevie Nicks on the radio and try to rationalize why I got the willies this morning when Zane greeted me with a hug and wouldn't let go. He pressed me to him, all of him, and I squirmed away to make small talk, and he didn't like it. Then again in the hallway, a half hour later. *You've got a dirty, suspicious mind, Molly* I told myself.

I turn up the music even louder and convince myself that I'm a sheltered little girl with an overactive writer's imagination.

11

I'm here at church, mingling and trying to dodge this guy who's been following me the past ten minutes. He was there at the coffee station, there in the book room, and there in the corner while I talked to Big Bill. Big Bill has been a regular, and I have seen him here since I was ten years old. He's barely an acquaintance and aptly nicknamed. He bent my ear with his latest philosophies of the natural order and our spiritual natures. If hitting on me was not part of his plan, I would have been into the conversation. "Molly, ah, I was wondering..." he said, smoothing his red goatee. "You're all grown-up now, and I'm single. Wanna, uh, get together sometime?"

"Bill, you're a great guy, but I'm taken," I said to let him down easy. He smiled, shrugged his shoulders, and retreated. I love older men, just not that one.

Then Stanley the archeologist saunters by. "Hi Molly. Wanna hang out sometime? I have some free time next week. Just came back from a dig and wanna share the experience with someone."

"Sure," I say. What to Hell. I already told him last month that I'm going with someone, and he said he just wants to be friends. I hope he keeps his word because I really would love to hear more about his work.

There he is again—the creepy guy who's staring a hole right through my head while he eats a doughnut. He pops the last bite into his mouth and dusts off the powdered sugar from his hands, and he's on his way over to me. "Hi. I couldn't help but overhear your conversation with Bill."

"What part?" I ask, a little shocked at my haughty tone.

"You were talking about astrology and the four elements Earth, Air, Fire, and Water. I think if I were an element, I'd be Earth. How about you?"

"Water, definitely."

"I think we'd be compatible," he decides, folding his arms across his chest. I suspect his straggly blond hair hasn't seen shampoo for two moons.

"Ah, let's see," I feign seriousness. "Put them together, and you've got mud." He doesn't get the hint.

"Ah, what's in all that stuff anyway? My name is Dan," he informs me. I look around for someone I know so I can excuse myself, but everyone's engaged in conversation.

Dad happens to walk by, and he mumbles something to the guy.

"Uh, I gotta go," the jerk announces out of the blue. He backs away nervously.

"Sure," I say with relief and then watch the guy make

his way around the room with a confused look on his face. "Hey Dad, what did you say to that guy?" I whisper.

"I told him to get lost," Dad answers flatly.

"Thanks." I laugh.

"See? You still need your father." He winks at me. I must admit, having a nosy father came in handy this time.

Speaking of fathers, Zane has been a choir boy since his last visit. No more creepy conversations or bad vibes. I chalked up his incest inquiry to his crazy knack of wanting to yank my chain. I plan on spending next weekend with him and Linda. Zane's friend Tony Catalano is having his annual art exhibit in the Poconos, and we are planning to take a spin by his opening to see what he's been up to.

I make my way out to the front of the church and sit down on the steps with a sigh.

I should have become a nun. Catholic nun, Buddhist nun, self-proclaimed nun. Part-time lesbian nun. Any kind of nun.

Stanley and I walk around the lake and chit chat. I had expected to hear all about his latest dig, but he's been evasive. "So, what's going on with you these days?" he asks.

"Well, now I teach two children's classes on Saturdays and one on Thursdays for older kids. It's going well."

"What else?"

"I've also been working on some writing. Trying to finish a book."

"So many interests. You remind me of a roulette ball circling around and around. It's like you are trying everything just to get in the hole," Stanley says as we sit down at the picnic tables.

"No, it's not like that at all."

"Explain it to me," he says. He looks me right in the eyes, and something doesn't feel comfortable anymore.

"I follow my abilities and passions. Creating is my life," I sum it up.

"You are a very complex woman." Stanley brushes his thumb against my pinky, and before I know it, he's lifting my hand to his lips. "Such soft skin."

"Stanley, you said you want to be friends," I say, trying to get my hand free without insulting him. But his lips start traveling up my arm, all the way to my shoulder. I don't want to rile him up because we are in a deserted place, and no one's in sight. If we were in a Greek myth, I'd invoke Artemis, and she'd stick an arrow up his butt. I wish I could do it myself. "Stanley, I have a boyfriend," I say, squirming away.

"Why didn't you say so?"

"We talked about this last month."

"We did? Where was I?" he asks with annoyance. He's not only rude, but he's senile.

"Yeah, we talked about it."

"No wonder why you're acting so nervous."

"You never told me about your dig. How did it go?" I ask, attempting to change the subject.

"I've gotta go," he says, checking his watch. He's pissed.

We say a quick goodbye, and I watch his car make clouds of dust on its way down the dirt road.

I throw a rock into the water. I should have known better. I'm so stupid.

I sit at the water's edge. The lake is a black mirror brushed with reflections—russet leaves, an old red barn, and blond grasses. The wind blows and smudges the palette of wet colors. I feel an ancient spirit here, something in the land that makes me feel as if it's poised between two worlds. Sometimes I wish I could slip into the world that's invisible to this one.

This lake reminds me of being fifteen and ice skating after meager snowfalls. I can still remember my skates cutting through soft white, gusts of wind enclosing me in snow dust. I would lean into an arabesque and glide inside a world of blowing crystal. I can still hear the sound of my skates and the raspy punctuation of blade against ice when I circled to a stop.

I wonder what this winter will bring. Mama and I dreaded Dad getting his license back earlier this month, but so far so good. He's still guzzling orange juice and eating a ton of apples now that the season is here. I've been baking for the local health food store, and I have been making extra for Dad. Since he's stopped boozing, he can put away half a dozen muffins a night. He seems to do everything in excess, and I feel guilty that it bothers me. I should just be glad he's sober.

Mama has faith in his sobriety, but I'm cynical. I would bet the farm that Dad will be rolling drunk by Halloween.

Speaking of Halloween, I hope to sneak some goodies to the kids this year. Every year Dad turns out the lights in the house to discourage pint-size revelers from knocking. Sometimes Dad's behavior convinces me that Scrooge has an evil twin brother.

Patty and I plan on going in costume to the nursing home to bring some levity to those who need it. Last year I saw a woman there who looked like me sixty years from now. She had the same bone structure and eye color. She kept asking to go home, and she didn't mean a place where she used to live.

I hope that by the time I am her age I won't be pissing my pants or still a doormat. Hopefully by then I will be able to kick some deserving ass and still look good in crimson lipstick.

Tony Catalano sure lives up to his reputation; everything he does is huge. This year he's rented a second-story warehouse in Milford, Pennsylvania for his three-day art exhibit. Zane and I make our way through his vast body of work, sometimes walking sideways to be able to access the next section.

"What do you think it's worth? You decide!" Tony says to a would-be buyer. He has his arms folded against his wide chest, and his denim shirt is stained with Prussian blue. He reminds me of an old Gypsy with his head of salt and pepper curls and his uncanny knack for bargaining with generosity and charm. One day he can charge a grand for a canvas, and the next day he can charge a hundred bucks for the same painting. Zane says it depends on how much good red wine Tony's had to drink. Whatever it is, I find him highly entertaining.

My eyes rest on a canvas that immediately takes me back to the Goddess retreat. A full moon ignites pastel clouds over an Impressionist forest.

And another, a simple boat drifting in the path of sunset on a canvas of exaggerated cobalt. Catalano's passion arrests me, and I long to throw away the graphic detail for the wild sweep of a brush, to do with canvas what Mama does with a song. "You think someday you are going to do a real painting, Tony?" Zane asks him half in jest, half in seriousness.

"And do you think that someday you'll get that brush out of your ass and loosen up a little bit?" Tony responds playfully. Their rivalry goes back to my early childhood. I can still hear them arguing about Realism versus Expressionism. I personally think they're jealous of each other for different reasons.

"Ah, never mind that, I want to introduce you to someone," Zane says, motioning for me to come over. "Remember my little girl?"

"Get outta town," Tony says and then narrows his eyes to inspect me. "Molly? That little girl who would kiss my cheek and I'd give her a five dollar bill? That little doll?"

"I guess that's me."

"I'll be damned. Emma sure did a good job. She sure is beautiful," he says to Zane.

"So darlin', do you like anything? Pick two paintings out. Tony and I will work out a deal," Zane says with a wink.

"Really?"

"You got it," Tony says. I motion with enthusiasm to the two canvases I was looking at.

Before I know it, Zane is loading them into the back of his Ford Blazer, and we're bouncing down the long stretch of highway back to Lackawaxen. "I can't thank you enough, Zane."

"For what?" Zane asks.

"For the paintings. For picking me up for the weekend because my car's in the shop. Everything." We grab hands, and Zane kisses my wrist with the enthusiasm of a little boy.

"You're welcome, Honeychild. And the weekend's only getting started. Tomorrow we'll take in some fall color, pick some apples, do some art."

"Sounds wonderful," I say, inhaling deeply as if I have just come up from deep water.

"What's going on at home?" he asks.

"Ah, nothing," I answer, avoiding the inevitable. "He's drinking again."

"I'm sorry."

"Me, too. Two nights ago he came home too happy. Not at all drunk, just a glint in his eye and a tone in the voice. I knew immediately. When I found the bottle in the garage..." I trail off remembering my knees buckling onto cold cement as I cried myself sick.

"Well you're here now, and we're gonna make the best

of it."

"Okay," I whisper, choking back tears.

The highway is a black ribbon winding through October gold. The sun sinks, splashing the trees in jewel tones.

"You know, I was all set to have a life with you and your mother. We planned you, right to the day," Zane says unexpectedly.

"I know."

"How much do you know?" he asks. He puts his headlights on as we ride into a mauve-tinted dusk. "I know we never really talked about this, but it feels right."

"I know you both adored each other."

"Molly, Tom's a good guy. But a simple guy. He could never understand your mother on any level."

"I know that."

"He hadn't touched her for years. He was a good provider, but not a real husband. Emma was half alive by the time we had met."

"She told me the same thing, though not in detail."

"I fucked it up. I knew I would," Zane says with vehemence. "I never forgave myself for letting another man raise my kid even if that's what he wanted and what we all decided."

"I'm sure everyone did their best at the time."

"Maybe some things work out the way they do for reasons we are not aware of," Zane muses.

"Did something remotely spiritual just come out your mouth? Zane Davis, you believe in something after all," I say, and he smiles.

"Don't read too much into it. But yeah, I believe in something."

"Tell me." Zane changes gears, and I hold onto the door to steady myself. This old Ford feels like we're coming in for a crash landing if we go over a pebble.

"I believe in Intelligence. And intelligences. I believe there are races out there far superior to our own. And Honeychild, I may love the beauty of this planet, but I sure as Hell don't feel like I belong here."

"You and me both. Did you always feel like that?"

"Yes."

"But you had a rough beginning. I think any kid would have felt like that."

"Yeah, maybe."

"How bad was it for you?"

"Well, my earliest memory is Christmas Day and my grandfather holding me by the ankles and banging my head against the floor because I spoke out of turn. It wouldn't be the first time. After Mother got sick and went into the facility, the orphanage felt like a refuge. But that didn't last too long."

"What was it like?"

"They were sadists, all of them. I remember them coming into the lunch room with platters of what looked like caramel. They told us we could have all the candy we wanted. Then we'd take a bite, and our throats would burn from lye."

"I'm sorry, Zane." I pause. "What about your father?"

"He walked out on Mother when she got pregnant. He

didn't want to marry her." He clears his throat. "Hey, I'm not the only one who has seen the worst of this world," Zane reasons. He slows down when he sees the glowing eyes of a doe ready to jet out into the road. "Your Mama is the most beautiful, pure thing I have ever known. She's too good for the likes of this world, including me."

"Zane..."

"It's the truth."

We fall into silence the rest of the way, each in our own bubble of thought. Every now and then the old Ford bucks, and I grip to stay in my seat.

I look forward to going back to his studio. My father's studio. It's the first time I have ever felt close enough to him to call him that even in my own mind.

It's a diamond-clear day, and the fields are humming with crickets. Zane and I circle the pond, keeping an eye out for turtles and if we're lucky, red-tail hawks. The pond's jagged perimeter creates a thick boundary of multi-colored grasses, ferns, and cattails; it reaches all the way back to the edge of the woods.

"I try to capture the pond in every season. My favorite time to paint is early spring, right when the peepers start singing, and the trees have the slightest haze of chartreuse. Umber, sap green, raw titanium, sienna. Colors almost good enough to eat," he says with a chuckle. Zane has the energy of a boy today. It's good to see a spring in his step.

"I'd love to paint the orchard," I muse. "Picking that fruit today made want to grab a brush and capture the cascading branches."

"Those knobby old apples? I think they're better for pies than paintings."

"No, I think the beauty is in the imperfection." Zane pauses and looks at me.

"This from a self-proclaimed perfectionist?"

"It's funny, but I celebrate imperfection around me but can't tolerate it in myself."

"It's all part of being human, Honeychild. Just as long as the self-criticism is constructive."

"And do you follow your own advice?"

"No!" Zane laughs. "Every morning I wake up to this decaying body and bald head and make the decision to either snarl or pray."

"Which do you settle on?"

"I don't pray so that leaves me with no other choice but to snarl." Zane gets me into a belly-aching laugh. "Don't mind this cynical old bastard," he adds. "Enjoy being young and hopeful, full of fire."

"I don't think I ever felt young," I admit. "Don't know why. I have always felt old in my head."

"That's because you're an old soul."

"I thought you didn't believe in souls."

"I believe in whatever it is that makes us...*us*. Call it what you will." Zane pauses. "I am glad of one thing, though."

"What's that?"

"That I'm not your age now. The world is more depressing than ever."

"Don't sound so hopeless. There's a movement of people rising up who care about what matters."

"Yuck, these neo-hippies make me gag. The recent Woodstock reunion proved how culturally bankrupt we really are."

"I thought you didn't like any kind of hippie, original or neo."

"I don't. But I sure as hell remember the intentions of some visionary folks during the Sixties. Overall, as a society, we were more inclined to do something, stand up against hypocrisy and strait-jacket authority."

"Whether you realize it or not, you and my parents were hippies."

"What?" Zane asks wide-eyed and getting uppity already. "Besides, we were over the hill, in our forties."

"All three of you left the city to get back to the land. You were an artist. Mama was a songwriter. She had an organic garden. Dad allowed you—even welcomed you—into their lives even after Mama knew she couldn't be with you. Come on, it sounds pretty counter-culture to me." Zane has to laugh.

"Well, minus the long hair, orgies, and drugs."

"Whatever." I roll my eyes and smile. Zane imitates me and tweaks my nose with his fingers.

"I loved Dylan, Cash, Baez, Patsy Cline. They don't make 'em like that anymore."

"Tell me about it," I say, dropping my voice when I spy

three turtles sunning themselves on a log.

"There was so much change going on when I met your mother. People of our generation in general have seen some amazing things. Horrible things. Beautiful things. I hate to think what you will see in your lifetime. I hope there is something beautiful in the muck."

"Things are changing; a lot's brewing in East Germany."

"Ah, the hell with all of it. This sky is too blue to waste it on talking about the world," Zane decides. "Let's see if Linda is baking those pies she promised us."

"Poor woman, all she does is cook when I'm here. She won't let me in the kitchen."

"That way she can drink while she's cooking. She's a pain in my ass," he growls.

"She says the same thing about you," I joke.

"Let me tell you something," Zane says, pointing his index finger in my face. His mood has just gone from jubilant to dead serious. "That woman wanted to marry me because she thought being with an artist made her special. Well, I'm nobody's trophy."

"I didn't mean to upset you."

"She only loves herself. And she wants me to be a trained monkey, to paint on cue. I knew what she was when I married her. I wanted a practical patron. It's convenience on both our parts."

"Whatever the reality, I think she loves you. I see how she looks at you, Zane."

"Don't side with my enemy!" he screams without warning. His face flushes into contorted disgust.

"Zane, calm down. I didn't mean to..."

"If you're going to survive this world, you have to understand human nature. You have to look beyond the pretty surface and see the motivation. Everyone has agendas."

"But you've got to trust somebody in this world."

"You have to educate yourself, goddammit!" Zane screams. "You need to read Gurdjieff to start with. It will change how you deal with people." I remain quiet. I know better than to voice my opinions if I don't want this to turn into World War III. "Bottom line is that you can't trust Linda. She will make you think she's your friend and then turn on you like a snake."

"Got it."

"All right. Sorry I got onto all that."

"Come on, let's see about those pies," I say as I begin walking back to the house. I tuck my scarf inside my jacket as the wind kicks up. Zane puts his arm around me. Within moments, he back to his jovial mood, but I'm still walking on egg shells.

"If Walt Whitman did it, it's good enough for me," Zane says after he shows me his layouts for a book of his art and anecdotes about life that he's in process of self-publishing. Like Whitman, he plans on selling copies from a knapsack and going door to door.

Many of his illustrations are charcoal self-portrait caricatures. They are zany and humorous, much like his real-life animated mannerisms. I forgive his volatile temperament and blame it on genius. "I think it's wonderful," I say with enthusiasm. "I love your thoughts and philosophy."

"Even the off-color jokes?"

"The whole package," I say. "I also appreciate page one-hundred ten."

"Ah...," Zane says, and his face softens. "You were only a few months old when I did that sketch."

"I love the quote beneath it."

"You'll find a lot of you and your mother in this book," he says with a touch of melancholy in his voice. "By the way, I read every page of your novel. It's good. Maybe too good. You sure you don't have a ghost writer?"

"Oh no, not you, too."

"You seem too sweet to write about all that complicated stuff."

"Sweet doesn't mean simple," I say.

"Speaking of sweet, I'm hungry again!"

"Hungry? After two bowls of Linda's beef stew and two slices of apple pie with a scoop of vanilla on each?"

"Let's raid the kitchen. She's probably asleep."

"You know, I could go for more of that delicious soup..." I raise an eyebrow. Zane jumps up from his chair, and I follow suit.

We giggle as we make our way downstairs. Zane puts a finger to his lips to be quiet so the dogs won't come barreling into the kitchen. I can hear them snoring like sailors in the living room. The house is pitch-dark, and

Zane turns on a dim lamp in the corner by the dining room table.

I rummage through the cabinets and fridge as quietly as possible. Zane stays on the other side of the narrow counter and rests his hands on his chin as he watches me heat up some stew. My mouth begins to water as soon as the gas flame starts to release its aroma. "Damn, I love food," I whisper as I lean into the utensil drawer. Just as my fingers grasp another soup spoon, Zane reaches over the counter and tweaks my breasts the way he tweaked my nose by the pond earlier today. But this tweak is slower, and no one's laughing.

The room starts to spin as my mind fills with noise and shuts down simultaneously. The only thing I can do is continue to mosey around the kitchen and convince myself that it didn't happen. "Did you see what I just did?" he asks, blowing that plan right out of the water.

"Uh, yeah..." I say slowly, methodically, almost with an air of dismissal.

"Well?"

"Well what?" I ask under my breath, avoiding his eyes.

"How do you feel about it? Was it good or bad?" he asks. My thoughts immediately scan the layout of the house for the nearest exit and remember that my car is back home in the shop. I turn off the stove and put on my bravest, unaffected face.

"Well, it all depends on the motivation behind it," I say, reflecting his words about human nature and psychology. I look him straight in the eye. He folds his arms across his chest and narrows his eyes as if trying to read me. His eyes feel like lasers trying to find a weak spot.

"Okay, okay. Very shrewd answer." He smiles slightly, but his eyes are still narrowed. He reminds me of a snake contemplating its next move. I pour some soup into a bowl as he uncrosses his arms and tries to lighten his tone.

"Would you ever model for me? I'd like to do a nude. I'd sit for you, too, if you weren't shy and wanted to paint this old heap of bones."

"Shy? No, not at all. You are my *father*, after all," I say with punctuation, looking him square in the eyes until he's the one who looks away, mumbling small-talk, something about the dogs and Linda.

"I'm too tired for another bite to eat. I'm turning in," he decides suddenly.

"Okay."

"See you in the morning." He disappears to the other side of the house, and I listen for the sound of the bedroom door shutting before I'm able to exhale. I pour the stew back into the pot and turn out the dining room lamp.

Only now do I feel my heart hammering under my ribcage; my hands tremble as I make my way upstairs to the studio.

I feel nothing. I think nothing. I try to remember nothing as I lock the door behind me.

12

The house smells like baked pumpkin, ham, and cloves as dinner cooks in the oven. Dad's watching television. He's like a fly trying to find a place to land as he flips through channels. "Screw the Berlin Wall. For chrissake, don't they have anything else to talk about?" he grumbles as he finally finds something that entertains him. "Now that's more like it," he announces when he discovers a World Wrestling Federation match. "Dinner will be done soon," I tell him. He ignores me or just doesn't hear me. I think it's the latter. "Dinner will be done soon!"

"What the fuck did you say?" he asks, pressing the mute button.

"I said dinner will be done soon. And I really think you need a hearing aid."

"I don't need any hearing aid. You mumble," he says as

he turns up the volume until I can hear Hulk Hogan pounce and grunt in every room in the house. "Fuckin' son-of-a-bitch, worthless cunt," he adds under his breath.

I rummage through the day's stack of junk mail and hope I don't find another card from Zane. I haven't seen him in a month and until today, have dodged phone calls as if they're bullets. He sends me cutesy friendship cards and signs them "Zane—from space." I don't appreciate the cards or the sarcasm.

We spoke on the phone this afternoon for the first time since...

I don't even know what to call it.

Detail by detail, drop after drop, with slow and steady constancy, it replays like a Chinese torture inside my brain. That night in the kitchen. The next morning. Both of us ignoring what had happened and how he went out of his way to start a nasty argument with me over something insignificant, something about spray adhesives to use over pastels. Linda looked at me and asked, "What's wrong with him?" I wanted to tell her everything, right in front of him. I wanted to tell his wife how he made a pass at his own daughter.

There, I've said it. There is nothing else to call it.

I sit at the kitchen counter and flip through a catalog as I try to stop thinking about that weekend. But my memory is like a kaleidoscope shifting in ugly patterns.

After the argument, his change in attitude and insisting I take a basket of apples home to bake a pie. Zane trying to give me a twenty dollar bill when he dropped me off and his words, "Come on, if you don't take it, I'll take off your blouse right here!" when I refused the money. He must have thought he was hilarious when he tossed the bill toward me and laughed through that stupid grin.

"If I did something to offend you, I hope you would tell me," he said on the phone today. I avoided the question. "You know, Molly, I think I've greatly overestimated your maturity."

"What do you mean?" I asked.

"Yeah, I've thought a lot about it, and I'm sorry to say that you are just little girl after all," he said and then hung up.

I throw down the catalog and pull my hair with frustration. If I were a little girl I would have screamed my head off that night in the kitchen and told the whole damn world what a degenerate he is. I would have told Mama so she'd go over there and shoot his genitals straight into space so Zane's signatures on those cards would hold some validity.

That's what would have happened if I didn't decide to sweep it under the rug. I'm scared to death of him. He's still like a land mine ready to go off at any time. God only knows what he'd do if his nose was rubbed into what he's pulled on me.

Mama once told me that before and after I was born, Zane told her in psychopathic detail how he was going to kill all of us because she wouldn't follow through on the life they had planned. He raged for years when Dad was at work and while I was at school or playing outside.

I remember days when he'd scream for eight hours at a time while my mother cowered at the table with a cup of tea, and he wouldn't let her get up to even go to the bathroom. She doesn't forget what he's capable of. Neither do I.

A part of me blames myself; if only I had been wearing a bra. If only I had questioned that conversation about incest a few months ago. If only I were a stronger person, he would have known he couldn't cross the line.

I wear a bra all the time now and ignore the fact that I have breasts at all. Mama says I look good in sweaters and form-fitting clothing, but I avoid anything that might bring attention to my chest. "Stand up straight," she reminds me, but I slouch so my breasts have no defining line and fade into the rest of me.

Dad startles my thoughts when he comes into the kitchen and starts stuffing his face with my latest batch of brown sugar muffins. His plaid robe hasn't seen a wash for God knows how long. I can smell it from here. The belt hangs loose exposing his naked parts. It's nothing new. When I was a little kid he walked naked around the house whenever he felt like it and pissed with the bathroom door wide open. "Tom, put some clothes on, will ya?" Mama snapped at him to no avail.

"Dinner's coming, and Mama will be home soon. Don't stuff yourself," I say with exasperation.

"Leave me the fuck alone," Dad barks through a mouthful of crumbs as he heads back to the living room. He turns up the volume even louder, and I go into the bathroom to escape.

I wash my hands, and my eyes snag my reflection in the mirror. The only thing that uncorks the demons inside my gut is to imagine a razor in my hand.

Deep and quick, the invisible blade cuts like lightning across my forehead, my cheeks. Into my chin, my mouth, my eyes and then my wrists. Cut out the poison. Carve my filthy, ugly self into oblivion until I bleed myself out.

Whole wheat blueberry-vanilla pancakes bubble on the hot griddle as I flip a red pepper omelet in the pan. It's my third week working as private cook for Ted and Christine Donahue. They live in the next town over with Gracie, their seven-year-old daughter. Ted is Mayor, and he and Christine are passionate vegetarians who are crazy about my healthy gourmet food.

I come to their house to make breakfast three mornings a week while Christine picks up dinners I prepare for them at our house. It works out well, and Gracie plans on joining my art classes soon.

I flip a pancake as she watches me with cocoa-brown eyes. "Wanna help?" I ask, and she nods with enthusiasm. We grasp the spatula together and make goofy girl noises each time a flapjack flips perfectly.

The Donahue kitchen is filled with collectible rabbits—porcelain, ceramic, wood, and metal—mostly antiques. They set a charming backdrop to a vast array of dried flowers and fruits including blushing hydrangea and tiny wild grapes. The scent of their house is a cross between a country florist and a fairy godmother's cottage. It is evident that peace lives inside these walls.

Sometimes I envy Gracie with her upright, sober Dad and wish that I had been kidnapped by normal people sometime before my first birthday.

Speaking of birthdays. Mama, Dad, and I went to Zane and Linda's to celebrate Zane turning sixty-seven. I avoid being alone with him these days and only visit him with Mama and Dad. But just when the tension in my gut starts to unwind a hair's breath, Zane manages to pull it even tighter.

We had just finished a midday meal, and we all took a stroll through the orchard to work off Linda's sinful mocha birthday cake. Zane brought his camera along and snapped some pictures of us under the trees. While Mama, Dad, and Linda were busy chatting in the courtyard, Zane insisted on taking pictures of me. *You son-of-a-bitch*, I thought when he demanded that I uncross my arms while he lectured me on body language. He said I come across as self-conscious and defensive. Gee, give the man a gold star. Zane took about six shots and then came over to me. "How I wish I was twenty years old and a stranger," he said quietly, resting his eyes on me. "My beautiful Molly. So much like your mother." Before his words could even penetrate my brain, he snapped out of his reverie and met up with the others. I felt sick inside.

Later that day, Zane told us that Dad took him aside and broke down crying. He asked Zane to take care of Mama and me if anything should happen to him. What a crock. As if Dad's taking care of us in the first place and Zane is capable of taking care of anybody but Zane.

I snap back to reality when Gracie clears away every last drop of maple syrup from her plate with her index finger and says, "More please!" through a sticky grin.

"You've had enough, young lady" Christine says and hands me the dishes as Gracie slouches down in her chair. "Don't worry. Molly is making your favorite banana bread tonight."

"That's right, Sweetie," I say as I wash the dishes and wipe down the stove.

"Thanks Molly, for taking such good care of us," Christine says right before I leave. I tell her it's my pleasure.

On the way to the car, I notice Bunny, Gracie's new horse in the stall. She's the color of butterscotch. Gracie runs out of the house with a handful of carrots and waves to me as Bunny trots over to the fence. The two greet each other in mutual admiration.

I get in my car and wonder if I'm too old to be adopted.

Dad still tanks up on booze when he goes out with us, but we still haven't found where he keeps his stash in the car. I am hell-bent on solving this five-year mystery.

I turn our Jeep Cherokee almost upside down looking for that God-damned bottle. Under the seats, the mats, glove box, tool case, even the first aid kit. Still nothing. I sit down on the back seat and sigh with exasperation.

And then I notice something I've never noticed before. Invisible from any angle but this one, a tiny leather loop tucked way under the back of the seat behind the seatbelt buckle. I get out of the car, lean over and give it a tug. It won't budge. I pull hard, harder until the whole seat lifts up. "Busted, Daddy Dearest," I say out loud when I rest my eyes on a half-consumed bottle of vodka nestled within the black metal coils of the seat's interior.

Now it all makes sense. How Dad can sit and get ossified drunk without a hint of evidence.

I take the bottle and stuff down the seat with all my might. I chuckle with glee as I watch the vodka gurgle down the drain. Next I go behind his tool boxes to his stash in the garage and dump it down the sink. After that I pour out the bottle tucked in the pocket of his Navy blue blazer inside his closet. I know he'll just get new bottles and new hiding places, but for now I feel accomplished, as if I'm doing one small thing to stop the hurricane.

And I don't care if all Hell breaks loose.

"God damn sons-of-bitches," Dad grunts non-stop when he discovers that his bottles have all been confiscated. "You have no fuckin' right!" he yells to no one in particular. It's one of the few times I've heard him actually yell instead of cursing under his breath.

"Okay, Tom, if you don't have a problem then why do you have bottles all over the Goddamned house?" Mama asks.

"That's my prerogative," he says, taking off his shirt to change clothes. The Old Bitch has summoned him to pick her up in New York tonight instead of Friday. It's good he's sober. As Dad takes off his shirt, Mom notices a Band-Aid-like patch on his right arm, just below the shoulder.

"What's that?" she asks. He pulls away violently when she tries to inspect it.

"None of your fucking business. Or that worthless bitch over there," he says as he scrambles to put on a shirt before Mama can get another look.

"You son-of-a-bitch, you call my kid that one more time, and I'll kill you. You better tell me why you're wearing that patch or I'll call Dr. Anderson and find out myself."

"You would do that, Emma. You're a cold-hearted bitch."

"What's the patch for, Tom?" she asks, ignoring everything that comes out of his mouth. I don't know how she turns a deaf ear and acts as if she's immune to his verbal filth. I may be used to it, too, but that doesn't mean I don't wanna punch his lights out. "What's it for?"

"It's none of your business."

"All right, I'll just call the doctor."

"Anderson's fucking crazy. He says it's for high blood pressure or some bullshit. Who cares!" Dad throws on a brown blazer and grabs his keys. "I'm moving into a fuckin' furnished room."

"Good! Be my guest!" Mama screams.

"Fuckin' bastards," he mumbles on his way out.

Schnapps runs for cover to get out of the way. "Get outta here you black bastard or I'll kill ya," he adds before slamming the door almost off the hinges.

"I know why you got rid of the bottles, but you shouldn't have done it," Mama says as she watches Dad disappear down the road. "It's only gonna make him worse."

"What could be worse?" I yell.

"Forget it, Molly. I'm too tired," she says and heads for the bedroom.

The Old Bitch is in New York. Mama and Dad are off, and it's my birthday. I'm looking forward to going out to eat somewhere. Nothing fancy, just out. "You want a glass of wine, Baby?" Mama asks when we decide which restaurant to choose from to celebrate my legal drinking age.

"Nah," I say, caring less. "But thanks anyway." We hug until we start laughing and Schnapps barks to get our attention. "You jealous dog," Mama says, giving him a pet.

Our plans to eat out are cancelled the minute Dad stumbles in the house. He's drunker than drunk and holding a present for me. "My baby, my lil girl. Twenny one years ol," he slurs with tears in his eyes.

"Tom, I begged you. Not tonight...why did you have to drink *tonight*?" Mama says. "I wanted to take the kid out." She starts crying. He barely notices.

"We will. Waz the pro'lem?" He smiles sweetly. He's

drunk, happy, and clueless.

"Never mind," I say, trying to keep the peace. The last thing I want is an argument.

I take the box from Dad and try to open it with enthusiasm. It's a brand new deluxe set of Rembrandt pastels. "Those are the ones, right?" he says, pawing my head in attempt to hug me. He's unsteady and can barely stand up. He almost falls off the kitchen bar stool, and I jump to help him before he goes down. I hug him and thank him. Tears are stuck in my throat; it feels like I swallowed a hot brick. "Dad, why don't you go lie down for a while?"

"Yeah, maybe yur right," he says as he attempts to get to the bedroom. "It's been a long day. I'm beat." Mama and I follow him into the bedroom, and he tumbles onto the bed. He's out like a light within seconds.

Mama wants to take me out to eat anyway, but I opt to just stay home. She says it's not right that we don't mark such an important birthday. I tell her it doesn't matter, and she starts crying again. The truth is that I don't feel like celebrating anything.

She hands me a small velvet box. Inside is a sterling Victorian-style locket, heart-shaped. "You are my heart," she says and hugs me as only Mama can.

"I'll treasure it," I whisper. She makes right whatever's wrong with the world, my world.

We end up getting Chinese take-out and watching a Neil Diamond video, his Greatest Hits Live, as rain blinds the windows.

Around midnight, I light my prayer altar and scribble a letter to myself to be opened in fifty years:

Dear Molly,
You will be in your twilight years when this letter reaches you. Perhaps you will be snow-haired, wearing a purple dress and sitting comfortably in your chair on a breezy day.
I do not know if you are bitter or content, alone or lonely, and I wonder if you take yourself as seriously as I take myself today. I wonder if you remember me at all...the dark-haired struggling artist who battles to keep her inner flame undaunted; how she envies the fireflies that blink in the blackness even when the night sleeps on a pillow of rain.
I yearn for your chair and your breezy day.
The sorrows that divide us make me wonder if we will ever meet; if I will be able to blink my light through all the nights that bridge you and me.
If the rains are nourishing, these words will find you accomplished and satisfied, and we will have a lovely afternoon tea together, reading poetry and watching memories dance in the breeze like grandchildren.
Until then, my sister-self, may the Fates bring us safely together. Wait for me.

I sign the paper, seal it in a pale blue envelope, and put it in a drawer where no one else will find it.

13

"I'm a rich man," Dad mumbled the night before last as he watched the cars go by. He sat at the kitchen table feeling cocky as if he had just made the Forbes list. Mama and Dad received some money from Mr. Bosco's estate after all. Twenty grand. The original amount was forty grand, but The Old Bitch put a stop to it before Mr. Bosco died.

Dad gave me two hundred bucks and kept throwing bills at me. "Come on, take more. I'm a rich man," he said and kissed me on the top of the head.

Now that The Old Bitch stays at The Essex House most of the week, Dad has a lot more time on his hands to get plenty drunk.

He's home today, and I'm having a nervous breakdown. My Thursday art class students are due to arrive in twenty minutes, and Dad is sitting in the car outside the garage crocked to the gills. It's ninety-five degrees. He's half passed out in the hot sun. "Dad, come on. You've got to get out of this heat. Come on in the house," I urge him. He looks at me from under his eye lids and tries to smile. "Doan worry abou it," he says. "I'm fine." He's thick-tongued and soaked to the skin with sweat. He nods off again, but this time his eyes roll up in his head.

"Dad, you're gonna get heat stroke." I open the car door and try to rouse him. His eyes flutter open again. "Dad, the kids will be here in fifteen minutes. Please, please get in the house."

"Wha kids?"

"My art class! Come on, if they see you drunk, I'm out of business. And you've gotta get out of this heat."

"Ah, ta hell with 'em all," he mumbles, falling back into a daze.

Ten minutes later, he's finally out of the car. He's holding onto me and walking an inch at a time into the house. He has all of his weight on me, but before I know it the heel of his shoe catches on the mud mat outside the door. He goes down like a ton of bricks, his legs bouncing up over his head. "Dad! Are you all right?"

"Yeah, yeah, I thin so," he slurs. He's on his back like a beetle in front of the side door, the same door the kids use, the door that everyone can see from the road and the driveway when they pull in. I have three minutes to get him up and pray to God that the kids are late. Samantha and her mom always get here five minutes early, and

Prima Donna Sunshine

they're due any minute.

"Dad, you've gotta grab my hand. One, two, three..." He's dead weight. He's too drunk to even turn over slightly so he can grab onto something. "Dad, one more time... one, two, three!"

"Leh me rest for a minna," he begs me.

"Try, please. Come on, one more time..." I plead as I hear a car pull into the driveway. It's Samantha and her Mom followed by Trish and her Mom. "Dad, grab my hand!" He grips my wrists with both hands, and on the count of three I pull him as if my life depends on it. I hear the sound of a car door and Samantha talking up a storm. "One, two, three!" I say to Dad and pull again.

Dad's finally on his feet just as Samantha runs toward the door. "Hello Molly. Is everything okay?" her mother asks when she sees Dad going into the house.

"Yeah, no worries. Dad has a frozen knee, and he took a spill. Just give me five minutes, ok?"

"Oh, sure. If you need anything, let me know," she says with a smile. Dad gives her a half-assed wave over his shoulder as he faces the door.

"Thanks!" Dad and I go into the house, and I get him into the bedroom as fast as possible.

"I'll just take a nap," Dad announces.

"Yeah, sleep for a couple hours," I say, making sure he's on the bed before I close the door.

I catch my breath and notice a pain in my low back, near the coccyx, but it's secondary to my fears of him waking up an hour from now and walking naked into the kitchen while the kids are busy at their desk easels in the living room.

I say a prayer and hope he sleeps like Rip Van Winkle.

Mama once told me about the time she felt adventurous in the kitchen and took home a lobster from the market. She said her bravery vanished when she looked into the pot of boiling water and realized what she was about to do. She didn't have the courage to throw the lobster in head-first, so it died slowly, arching its back in repeated shocks. She said she never forgot the incident or forgave herself for being such a coward.

I think Dad is Mama's lobster. I think leaving him would be like throwing him into a pot of boiling, sobering water, and she just can't do it.

Today is one of those days when compassion for Mama having compassion for Dad is getting old. I'm walking through the cemetery trying to cool off. Mama and I rarely argue, but today we almost blew the roof off the house.

I told her I can't take my life anymore. She told me she can't hear it right now, that one more thing to worry about will push her over the edge. I told her she doesn't have to worry about me. She told me it could be worse, that he could beat us, that he could be jobless and in the gutter. I told her it could also be a helluva lot better. She told me she can't deal with my pain right now. I told her I'd have a life if she hadn't raised me to be just like her, a shit-eating doormat. She told me that I owe Dad because he raised

Prima Donna Sunshine

me even though I'm Zane's kid.

I shudder to think about the words that came out of our mouths, especially mine. Mama spent her entire life sacrificing for my well-being. I would trade all of the sacrifices for one and only one: that she'd leave Dad on the floor, in the dark, and never look back.

I notice a head stone that reads Tiger Cat Farm. It marks the resting place of the tight-lipped farmer who murdered his family and then killed himself. Flowers crown his name, and the grass is trimmed. The stone next to his belongs to the old lady who died in a nursing home making holiday ornaments for ungrateful girl scouts who only visited her to get badges on their uniforms. She sleeps beneath weeds and doesn't even have a decaying wreath from last Christmas.

In my mind, I search for my father here. I clutch a bouquet of flowers and apologies for having grown to hate him. But then I remember that he hates flowers as much as he hates giving or taking apologies.

He has to be here, I muse; he sure isn't amongst the living. I ask the angel carved in stone if she's seen a burnt-out man bled of the humor my child-self once loved him for, but the angel withholds her reply.

I pick a buttercup and play the childhood game; I hold the flower beneath my chin and wonder if there is a bright reflection. They say the petals give you their gold if you're beautiful. Since there is no one else around, I ask the angel if she sees a reflection under my chin. She gives me silence once again, like my father who never saw a reflection on my face, either.

Dad must be somewhere near the farmer; they have a lot in common. One killed his family deliberately with a gun. The other did the job with a bottle and without intent. They are probably stumbling together down the hallways of Hell, arms linked, laughing and crying in their shot glasses about how the world misunderstood them.

I snap out of my cynical reverie and study the names etched in stone. Only by their sins are the dead remembered.

Everyone overlooks the sweat-drenched days a husband labored to support his five kids, but they remember he had a mistress on Maple Street. They disregard the mistress who devoted her life to battered women because she had been one herself. They forget the people she cried and healed with, but God dammit, they remember who she slept with.

They discredit the spinster's four published books and the degree that states she was the first woman in her time and town to go to college. But they remember her woman lover and the children she never had.

Names etched in stone, cold and fameless here in the grass but unforgotten in the gossip that goes around the table with the mashed potatoes.

Well, Dad, you don't sleep in this graveyard, and you don't breathe with the rest of us out there beyond the heavy iron gates and the shrewd smiling angel in her granite garment. I guess you're drifting in the cemetery for people who choose the in-between world, the safe, enveloping bottle that numbs heartache and puts out humor.

I'll leave a bouquet of apologies for the old lady who now has the last word over the snickering girl scouts. I'm sure she loved flowers and deserves an apology.

Dad, half-crocked, went to bed early, so Mama and I decide to take a drive. We pack up peanut butter waffles and Schnapps and head to the waterfall on the back road.

The moon scalds the water platinum, and the cascade drifts out in bell-like tones gathering in eddies beneath the willow trees. "Baby, forgive me. Forgive my selfishness today. I was at the breaking point. I want you to know that I'm here for you, always. No matter what, no matter how hard the truth is to hear," Mama whispers. I give Schnapps a bite of waffle and watch him gulp it down as he sits sphinx-like on the back seat. "And you don't owe Tom anything. You are an innocent child who was brought into a complicated situation."

"I'm sorry, too. I just snapped. I don't mean to make it harder for you." We hug and hold each other as if we're standing at the edge of the world, a blade of precipice that could swallow our sanity whole at any moment.

"He's gonna die. He's gonna die whether we enable him or let him go. I just can't have it on my conscience if he dies because I abandoned him. Underneath it all, he's a lost soul. He had so much potential, Molly. I remember."

"Patty says that we all have potential," I say.

Mama stares out at the black and silver water as she sips from her thermos. "Tom smoked almost three packs of cigarettes a day, but when he read an article about the ill effects of cigarettes, he crushed out the cigarette he had in his mouth and never smoked again. I still have faith he will do that with the booze. I know he can do it."

"He doesn't want to do it, and that's how I know he will never get help."

"I have to see him through, Honey. I loved him since I was sixteen years old." She pauses. "He was the one who picked up the pieces for my brothers and sisters after Mama drank herself to death. He helped to get some of them sober when they became drunks, too." Tears shimmer in her gray eyes. "I married him because he was sober, so together. He didn't drink, never cursed. I can't believe he's turned into what I thought I had escaped all those years ago."

"I know," I say, holding back tears in the dark.

"I don't expect you to see him through."

"No, but I'm gonna see you through. I love you, Mama." I lean my head on her shoulder, and Schnapps peeks out from the back seat. He licks my shoulder, his way of asking for another bite of peanut butter waffle. We start laughing and hand him small bites so the peanut butter won't get stuck on the roof of his mouth.

Mama puts on the radio. A reverend has an inspirational program each night at eleven, and the final half-hour segment is ending. "If you find yourself lost in a dark sea tonight, being tossed from one terror to another, know that God has made a harbor for you that is a prayer away," he says in a soft voice.

Part of me is cynical, and I roll my eyes. But then Mama and I grasp hands and listen to his comforting words.

We close our eyes and say our own prayers. The thunder of the waterfall is a silver litany in the night, and for this moment, we have hope again. And it is enough.

Kate and I ran into each other at the market last week. It's been ages since we've talked or taken a walk, and I was happy to see her. She introduced me to her friend by saying, "This is my friend Molly. Well, she's really too young to be my friend."

Too young to be her friend, but not too young to be her shrink, I thought.

Or too young to be Jake's new girlfriend. Little does the beautiful bitch know that I haven't been able to get rid of him since I met him by chance at the health food store. He buys my cranberry muffins like they're going out of style, calls to chit chat about writing and drops by unexpectedly just to say "Hi." He whines about his lack of dating prospects and waits for any hint that I want to jump his bones. His ego is repulsive, not to mention his beard that needs an appointment with a turbo-charged weed whacker.

Yesterday I had PMS cramps from Hell and a severe case of Drop Dead, Jake. The doorbell rang when I was still in my night clothes, and the last thing I wanted to do was feel obligated to answer it. Schnapps did his usual attack performance, springing against the door in an attempt to get rid of the guy who just can't take a hint.

Jake rang the bell three times before he started knocking like a kid who wanted a candy bar after the store closes. Instead of figuring no one was home or he had come at a bad time, he proceeded to tap on the kitchen windows while he peered in like an impatient yeti. I knew this because I could see his reflection on the oven door as I peeked into the kitchen from the hallway. It took him ten minutes to finally give up while Schnapps growled and slobbered his disapproval all over the front door.

The phone rang a few hours later. It was Jake. "Next time I stop by, I'd appreciate it if you didn't pretend you weren't home. Just answer the door," he commanded before he hung up. The guy, as Dad would say, has more balls than a brass monkey. And I have the chutzpah of an ostrich sucking up sand.

Speaking of ostriches. One of Zane's acquaintances from his Monday night writer's group has commissioned me to illustrate a children's book about an ostrich. Lizzie, the author, is a lady in her sixties with a sweet smile and a good helping of sweet Southern drawl.

She also thinks that Zane is the greatest thing since sliced bread. "You are so fawtunate to have Zane for a fawther," she says. I just smile, complete my chapter assignments, and cash her checks.

The money is coming in handy since I've been going to a chiropractor three times a week to stop this lightning pain shooting down my right leg. I've had to cancel some of my art classes and cut back on cooking for the Donahues because of it. "Any accidents or heavy-lifting?" the doctor asked me when he noticed compressed discs on the x-ray.

"Probably moving furniture," I lied when I really wanted to say, "One hundred-ninety-five pounds of drunken old man."

This sciatic pain is unbearable not to mention my jaw that tends to lock in the mornings. I've been drinking protein shakes through a straw because I can't get a fork in my mouth. Loyalty, co-dependence, stupidity—whatever it is that keeps me here should be summed up in one word: masochism.

Patty and I tape up the last two boxes for her move and glance around her living room. Most of her belongings will be donated to The Salvation Army. It's her last night here, and my heart is already broken. "Hey, Sweet Pea, look what I found in a magazine the other day," she says, handing me a folded article. "It's all about Native philosophies, Shamanism. I couldn't help but remember that experience you had while on retreat last year. From what I've read, I think that spirit woman was some sort of teacher."

"I still can't see what she meant; the only age I seem to be entering is the age of insanity, not power." I try to laugh.

"Well, hold your horses. In Tribal cultures, power is only

gained through severe testing."

"I'll keep that in mind," I say with the enthusiasm of a sloth. "Okay, say I'm chosen for—whatever the hell it is—and then what?" I spread my arms and feign gratitude. "Besides, if co-dependency was a spiritual calling then the world would be overrun with shamans."

"You got that right," Patty says, giving in to a hearty laugh before turning serious. "I just wish you'd pull out of the situation and let your father fall. I know you love your mother, but you can't live their lives."

"It's nothing I don't tell myself every day."

"But I respect your choices. I love you for you. And I'm gonna miss you," Patty says as she grabs me in a hug. We start crying and laughing. "You'd love Hawaii. I see you painting on the beach and hanging out with such creative and spiritual people. Please visit."

"I'll try." I stuff the article in my pocket and take a deep breath. "I love you, Patty."

"Aloha, Honey Bun."

And that's the last thing she says to me. I hand her a poem I've written for her departure and get in my car before I start sobbing and make an ass out of myself.

I open the window and cry against the wind as my tires crunch and scatter dry leaves along the road.

I think about transience. Autumn leaves, passion, epiphanies, dreams, ideals. Their purity lights upon our lives like birds on new snow. Then the years and the winds blow over them leaving no proof that they were ever here at all. Beauty is only a visitor, and then she is gone.

14

It's nearing one in the morning. Mama and I are still at the VFW Halloween party. Mama wanted to bail out on coming here tonight because she was too tired and burnt out. She had no idea what costume she would wear so I suggested she come as she feels: ready for bed. Bathrobe, slippers, curlers in her hair. "Go all the way," I said and got her a green mud mask for her face and a soap opera magazine to tuck into her pocket. We laughed like crazy at the end result.

I decided to go as an artist with a paint-stained poet's shirt, beret, and a palette swinging over my shoulder.

It's good to see Mama having a good time. She's sitting at a table and talking to Dracula, Peter Pan, and a hooker while I dance my heart out. I can't believe she decided to leave Dad home alone to watch his wrestling matches and drink to his heart's content. She said it will be his problem if he ends up on the floor. I couldn't agree more.

I'm glad I decided to wear these comfortable, old carpenter boots so I can dance another hour. I don't care if I wake up crippled with back pain tomorrow. Tonight I'm going to be young even if it kills me.

The guy across from me is dressed as a nun, and girl to my right is creepy in her tarantula costume. There's a cute guy in a toga who's been giving me the eye all night, but I turn off any hint of interest and keep an eye out for any lesbians.

I realize how quickly the universe answers requests when a butch in plain clothes cuts in front of the tarantula to dance near me. I also realize I should have been specific. *Lipstick lesbian, please.*

I make an attempt to shimmy in another direction, but it's too late. "Hi there," she says in a voice surprisingly tinged with helium and barely audible over the noise.

"Uh, hi," I say, trying not to look interested without being rude.

"I'm Deanna." She smiles and gives me a look as if she's craving ice cream and I'm cherry vanilla.

"Molly," I shout over the music and pretend to get into the song and my own space.

"I like your costume."

"Uh, thanks."

"I like your boots," she says with a wink.

"Just for comfort, to my boyfriend's dismay!" I lie and actually believe it. Her smile wanes, and it isn't long before she dances in another direction.

The beat of the music pulses through my chest and

under my feet. My mind drifts back to Dad; he better not be on the floor. I decide I'm having too much fun to worry about it when the guy in the toga comes over and dances next to me. "Carpe diem!" he shouts over the music. He gives me a big smile. I give him thumbs up.

Yes, seize the day. That's exactly what I plan to do from now on.

They're right when they say that if you want to hear God laugh, just tell Him your plans. I planned on letting go of some seriousness and toxic loyalty to less-than-deserving people.

Then Zane dropped the bomb. "I have prostate cancer. With radiation treatment, they give me three to five years," he informed matter-of-factly. "The only thing that gets me is that I won't see the new millennium come in."

Despite everything, the news went through me like an arrow. I cried while Zane stood in front of me with a stoic face. "I'll have none of that," he said. "Come on, let's make the best of what we've got. I just want to spend more time with you, Honeychild." He softened. We hugged, and from that moment on, we simply started over.

He's been coming over on Tuesdays again. We go out to lunch and order shrimp salad and chocolate cake and laugh so loud we're surprised we don't get thrown out of the restaurant. We talk, read poetry, and go through his journals from World War Two while we perch on a picnic table by the lake.

Even with a catheter inserted into his abdomen to drain his bladder, he manages to maintain his humor. He breaks into crazy antics each time he excuses himself to empty his urine bag, and for a minute, I forget he's sick. I like to think the worst is behind us, and we can truly be father and daughter for however much time he has left.

I've been dabbling with my manuscript again, treading water more than writing but at least it's an attempt. To Zane's dismay, I've ventured into what he calls "fantasy painting." It's a series of pastels based on personal mythology with an emphasis on strong women and goddesses. *The Fire Gypsy* is my favorite. Her mane of red hair flames into fire, and she holds a tambourine. In essence, she's a gorgeous, dangerous bitch, and I love her for being what I'm not.

The parents of my students and I rented the local community hall to present the children's first art exhibit. With a potluck table, an open mic for poetry and singing, and overall fun, the evening was a success. Jessica, my talented ten year old student, stole the show with her Mary Cassatt-style watercolors.

The Fire Gypsy turned some heads, too, mostly men. It never ceases to amaze me how a lot of men love long hair on women, even in paintings.

I had enough of Jake the Jack Ass commenting on my own long hair and decided to chop it to shoulder-length. I've also, for now, surrendered to its straight, natural dark brown with Cleopatra bangs.

There's a cute new boutique a few miles out of town,

and I indulged in some Christmas shopping today. The boutique is an old Victorian dolled up with fragrant evergreen over the doors. The owner played Shaker music and burned beeswax candles while the first snow flurried against the window panes. I bought patina wind chimes for Mama, the kind that sound like monastery bells—and a great conversation piece for Dad—a perfect miniature of a biplane that also functions as a cigarette lighter. I know it's no longer a reality, but I know he still dreams of taking flying lessons.

Happy with the day's simplicity, I've made a special dinner of roasted chicken stuffed with Moroccan couscous, apples, cranberries, and fresh sage. Dad has been perfectly sober all day, but I think he downed a considerable amount of vodka before he sat down at the table.

I try not to think worry about it as we all eat in relative peace. No Television, rants, cursing, slurring, and not even a word about The Old Bitch. Maybe we're in the Twilight Zone.

I take a second helping of gingered carrots and Dad raves about the meal and gives me a sweet smile. Mama agrees with him and gives my hand a squeeze. "Honey, since The Old Bitch will be in New York until Friday, I was thinking that we all take a drive to the Poconos. I don't know, it might be nice to see the old stomping grounds," she says to Dad.

"That sounds great," I comment as I slice some chicken breast.

"Honey?" Mama asks, but Dad remains quiet. "Tom?" I look up at Dad and realize he's staring into space with the fork falling out of his hand. "Tom!"

I rush out of my chair and shake his shoulders, but he gives me no response. Dad loses consciousness within seconds and slumps head-on into his plate. "Call an ambulance!" Mama screams as she rushes over to him. I can barely breathe as my shaking fingers try to dial 911. I dial the wrong numbers. "Tommy, wake up! Tommy, oh God..." Mama slaps his face and does everything to revive him but to no avail. "Hurry up, Molly!" I dial again.

An emergency operator comes on the line and takes down my stammered information. "Miss, we are sending out an ambulance immediately. Try to remain calm," she says.

Dad comes to a few minutes after I hang up the phone. He's violent and acts like he's possessed by devils. He goes nuts when Mama tries to tell him that he had lost consciousness. "Geh outta here," he slurs but it's not from booze. It's something else. He's like a madman as he takes his dinner plate and heaves it across the kitchen floor. It shatters as a chicken leg and carrots go flying. He tries to stand up with effort. "Don't tell me you called an ambulance, you bastards! There's nothin' wrong with me! If anyone comes in this house, I'll shoot their fuggin' brains out," he raves with blazing eyes.

"Tom, calm down. Just let them check you out. You're slurring, and you're not walking right. Come on, let them check you out!" Mama pleads with him.

Ten minutes later, an emergency technician knocks on the door. Dad stumbles toward it as if he's out for blood. "Get outta here!" he howls. Mama pulls on his shirt to hold him back and slips between him and the door so she can answer it. "Get outta here now!" Dad screams again. "I'll burn the house down if you open that door. I swear, Emma!" Mama hesitates as the knocking continues. I push past her and go outside to deal with it.

"I'm sorry to bring you guys out, but all seems okay. Don't mind him, he had a few drinks. Everything's fine," I smile, putting on my life-is-a-bowl-of-bonbons face.

"Miss, it's our obligation to check out the scene and take vitals," one man says. I can see how blue his eyes are each time the ambulance lights flash from the driveway. He's professional and well-meaning, but there is no way I can let him in this house. Dad's ranting can be heard from the kitchen. The EMTs looks concerned.

"He's harmless," I say. "And fine, as you can tell. He's back to his crazy self," I lie and force a laugh to ease my embarrassment as the profanity reaches a feverish height.

"Alright, but I need you to sign here." He hands me a clip board and marks an X where I should put my signature. I scribble my initials and thank him for his prompt response. He nods and walks away with hesitation. I'm relieved when I see them drive away.

Dad's still ranting like a lunatic when I walk back in the house. "Tom, I think you had a stroke. You better get checked out," Mama pleads with him.

"Screw you!" he yells and puts on the TV.

Mama and I stare at each other. "I've never seen him like this. Something happened to his brain, I know it," she whispers to me.

"Well whatever it is, we'll never get him to a doctor."

"I know that," Mama says, choking back tears. I hug her and then proceed to clean up the kitchen floor. My heart is still pounding from adrenaline as I sweep shards of broken plate and food into a dust pan. Mama clears the table. "Baby, I'm so sorry. Such a beautiful dinner." She breathes as if the world is on her chest.

"I should have expected it. The day was too good," I say as I glance into the living room. Dad's watching the wrestling match with his hand cupped to his deaf ear so he can hear it better. He's back to his indifferent self, wrapped in his own mumblings about how the world is out to get him.

I should be worried about him. I should try to encourage him to see a doctor and get checked out. I should go over to him and ask how he feels, even if he bites my head off.

For the first time in my life, I simply don't care.

It's a warm Thursday morning in May, and I'm coming back from Zane and Linda's. Zane received the first shipment of his book, and he's already scheduling readings and local book signings.

He's also looking haggard with sunken cheeks. He sat for me while I did a charcoal of him in his denim shirt. He told me about his radiation treatments as he scowled and knitted his brows. "Don't make me pretty. Real art never lies," he said. And so I didn't.

Mama asked me to stop by before I go shopping for the Donahues' party. She said it was important but I'm already running late. At least The Old Bitch is in New York this week, and she won't be grilling me about my work or my love life.

Speaking of. Fred Bolinsky, a kid I knew in high school looked me up and now sends me book-length letters and pictures of himself in his Army uniform. He also sends me shots of himself bare-chested on the bench press. I think he's certain that this will turn me on. He also has an arm full of badly-rendered ink, and his latest tattoo is supposed to be a jaguar. I gather that his tattoo artist was drunker than he was.

Fred was the nerdy kid in my eighth grade biology class who snorted when he laughed, never took notes and made the Dean's List, and always told mindless, obscene jokes. A fellow outcast, I was the only one who pretended to get his humor. He's been in love with me since then, or so he says.

Despite my detailed monologues about how I just want to be friends, he comes to New Blair when he's on leave and brings me flowers and jewelry. We go eat Chinese and see a movie. Zane thinks we're getting it on, and the Old Bitch, too. Hey, whatever. Sometimes it comes in handy when I want to shut them all up.

"Hi Baby," Mama says when I walk into the Bosco's

kitchen. We hug, and the wet dish towel over her shoulder falls on the floor. I pick it up for her, and she leans close to me. "Your father's half-crocked," she whispers.

"Ah, damn!" I am already fuming. "It's ten in the morning!"

"He has something he wants to tell you..." She winks. "I think it's about Zane." I run my hand through my hair. This is the last thing I need. "Go on, he's in the garage. Don't be too hard on him. I think he had to get drunk to tell you."

"Why now? After all these years?"

"He says he doesn't think he'll be around much longer." I can't help but roll my eyes. Mama pats my shoulder. "Go on, he's torturing himself."

Dad's so red in the face he's bordering on purple. I walk into the garage and try to not let him know that I notice he's been crying. "Yo," he says with a cute expression.

"Hey Dad," I say, giving him a hug. His big hands lock onto my shoulders and don't lighten up even when we part a few inches.

"You have a good time with that moron?" he asks, referring to Zane.

"Yeah, okay I guess."

"I got somethin' to tell ya and ya gotta listen to me..."

"I'm listening." I pat his shoulder to calm him down. He's sweating buckets.

"That son-of-a-bitch pansy artist," he says but trails off. "I'm tryin' ta say that I'm not...." His blood-shot eyes tear up again, and he's still holding me by the shoulders in a death grip.

"Yes you are." I say, looking him square in the eyes.

"No, you doan understand," he slurs. "I'm not yur father."

"Dad, yes you are."

"That crazy bastard is," he blurts out, spitting me in the eye unintentionally.

"No, he's not. I have only one father and that's you," I whisper.

"What? I can't hear ya," he says, cupping his ear with his hand and catching himself when he gets too unsteady.

"Dad, I know about Zane. I've known for years."

"What?"

"I just knew, okay?"

"Do ya love the bastard?"

"Not the way I love you. You're my only father and always will be. You hear me?" Dad starts sobbing. He shakes his head from side to side and smiles. He puts his wet face into my shoulder and holds onto me.

"I love you," he mumbles into my shirt. "My lil girl." He cries like a baby. "I doan deserve you."

"I love you, too, Dad. I want you around for a long time. Please try to stop boozing."

"I will. I promise." He pulls away from me and takes out his cotton handkerchief from his pocket. He steadies himself and blows his nose. He sounds like a drunken moose, and I have to laugh. He smiles at me and shakes his head. "I can't believe you already knew."

"None of it matters." We hug again, and he sobs for another round. His shirt is soaked; he's drunk as can be;

his nose is dripping into my hair and maybe he doesn't deserve me, but I don't want to let go. He's my Dad.

15

Eight-year-old Tabitha has just painted both her arms up to the elbows with green tempera paint, and the rest of the girls are giggling up a high-pitched rally to cheer her on. "I'm next!" Jessie screams with glee, reaching over the craft table to grab the big bottle of red poster paint.

"I want blue!" Lisa decides.

"And I want you in the bathroom right now under soap and water!" I say in a scolding voice. "And the rest of you, don't even think about it." The girls know I mean business and try to stifle their laughter. "I want this assignment finished. You have ten minutes." The students check the clock and get back to work like busy squirrels while I march Tabitha to the bathroom.

"I was just being creative, Molly," she says and looks up at me with puppy dog brown eyes. "You always tell us to be creative."

"Try to put it on your paper next time, okay?" I help her dry her arms with a towel, and she starts to giggle. A reluctant smile escapes my mouth, and her giggle expands into a loud laugh.

The other girls are singing New Kids on the Block and finishing up their projects when Tabitha and I walk back into the living room. "Joey is *so* cute," Gracie squeals, and the other girls follow suit. She looks up at me and asks, "Molly, do you have a boyfriend?"

"Maybe."

"What's his name?" Tabitha asks.

"Fred," I mumble, feeling pathetic.

"Fred!" Jessie yells, unable to restrain her distaste before laughing.

"What's wrong with Fred? We had a dog named Fred, a long time ago," Justine says.

"Enough about Fred. Four minutes and time's up for projects. Get cracking!" I say, wondering what their mothers would think if they knew that their art teacher is a closet wanna-be dyke. A part-time chicken dyke.

My wanna-be days just might be over. I look up from the stove in the Donahue's kitchen to see a pretty redhead. "Hi, I'm Lynn Thompson. We've here for the Donahue gig." She smiles and jostles her guitar case.

"I'm Molly. Go down the hall and take a left. We're setting up the party in there. Christine's around here somewhere," I say, glancing over my shoulder as I continue to chop vegetables.

"Thanks. Hey, something smells real good. Vegetarian?"

"Yup."

"Cool!" she nods and gives me a Julia Roberts smile. Just then a long-haired guy comes through the door carrying an amp and another guitar case. "Hey Babe, down the hall and take a left," she says and then turns to follow him. "Thanks, Molly!"

Hey babe, I repeat to myself sarcastically as I check my trays of zucchini parm in the oven then go back to my three huge wooden bowls of salad. Each one is an edible mandala in progress that would make rabbits swoon.

Tedious as sand paintings, my salad designs fan out like colorful tie-dye. Shredded raw beets, carrots, and turnips, sliced red and yellow bell peppers, three kinds of lettuce, pale green apples, artichokes, purple cabbage, pumpkin and sunflower seeds, dried cranberries and coconut, and edible spring flowers. Sure to please Christine and Ted's gourmet vege tastes.

The party gets into full swing, and the Donahue's thirty-five guests devour my feast like there's no tomorrow. I keep the food coming single-handedly and listen to Lynn and her boyfriend rock the house with their honey-toned blues. The guy looks flea-bitten, and I wonder what she sees in him.

I excuse my way to the buffet table to set down another soup tureen and catch Lynn out of the corner of my eye. She's purring into the mic and looking right at me. She winks slowly and then flashes Julia Roberts again. I do something out of character and downright unthinkable.

I wink back.

Over the past two months, I have burned more meals for the Donahues than I can count and feel that sometimes I have to remind myself to breathe. Mama hounded me for weeks and insisted that I tell her what's wrong with me. I finally broke down and told her my feelings for women. At first she was expressionless and out of words, except for, "Whatever happened to Neil Diamond?" We both ended up laughing and having an hour talk over a pot of tea. "My Baby, I don't know what to tell you. This world is cruel to anyone who loves differently. I don't want to see you suffer."

"And I don't want to suffer the way you have by loving so-called normally. Love is love, and love hurts, dammit."

"Are you gay?" Mama asked me point blank with a flicker of disappointment in her eyes.

"I don't know. I don't see gender. I could love anybody, but would prefer a woman," I confessed.

"There are a lot of good men out there, Molly. Wonderful men."

"Then why aren't you with one of them?" I asked without hesitation.

"We can't help who we love," she answered and then added, "And no matter who *you* love, I just want you to have a chance to be happy. I want to see you with someone you deserve, someone with the same heart." She touched my cheek, and we hugged for a long time.

We haven't spoken about it since, but every once in a while, she glances over at me to see my reaction when a pretty woman walks by. She does the same thing when a cute guy walks by. Usually we end up laughing.

It's a sweet distraction from the bitter reality here at home.

Mama and I had to call the ambulance two times this summer because Dad was in an alcohol stupor. They took him to the hospital, pumped him with fluids and then sent him back home the same damn day. All we wanted was one night to sleep and not worry about him, one night where he'd be in a place where he can't get any booze.

Two weeks ago, Dad was working in The Old Bitch's garage with her screaming at him about disorganized boxes. It was almost a hundred degrees, and he became unresponsive and keeled over, just like that night last winter when he fell headlong into his dinner plate. Mama called the ambulance, and they took him in for evaluation. The tests revealed more than one mini stroke. After Mama told the doctor how much he's been boozing, the doctor told Dad in no uncertain terms that he is headed for a major stroke if he doesn't stop drinking.

No doctor's warning, no amount of shame, Mama's crying or my yelling makes him want to get help. He's hell-bent on killing himself. I'd like to kill him myself, more times than I can admit to.

Yesterday the three of us resurrected World War II.

Mama and I screamed like wild women while Dad calmly told us to drop dead and to screw ourselves first.

And then he told me to go back to my "father's house."

The loving confession about Zane has now turned into a subtle weapon that he whips out when he wants to punish me because I'd like to see him sober.

After he said it, I stormed out of the house and ran down the road in my bare feet, crying until I couldn't see an inch in front of my face.

My thoughts are beyond my control sometimes, and I wonder what evil lurks inside the recesses of my soul. Sometimes I imagine Dad choking on the dinner I make for him. Choking, turning blue and dropping dead with my gourmet food stuck in his windpipe. Other times I imagine kicking him until every filthy word he's ever called me freezes on his cold, dead lips.

Then I imagine him sober, years ago, and I want to throw my arms around him and cry from remorse.

Most of the time I just think about doing myself in. I have it all set. I'll just find a reason to go to The Old Bitch's penthouse and jump out the window. Fly like a crazed angel in sunset light into the hard, unyielding mercy of the concrete.

Right now, Dad's sitting on the green metal chair next to the barbeque, and I'm trying to make an effort to ease my guilt by spending time with him. I notice that the rose bush on the trellis has died. It once had velvet blooms so deep a red they teetered on black. I was thirteen when we moved here, and that rose bush was my favorite thing about muggy New Jersey summers.

It's almost a decade later, and I can't help but think about the dreams we all had when we first moved to New Blair. Dad had planned on taking flying lessons at the local airport. Mama was going to record her album with a local band. And I was going to go to the private school perched on the hill overlooking Main Street.

August heat and unexpected downpours have left the driveway steaming like lava, and the sky is the color of lemons. Needles of light pierce the scrawny cedars that partially shield our house from the road. Dad's quiet, half-lit but coherent. I want him to ask me something, anything. About my classes or my job with the Donahues or any other mundane thing. He never once asked me about my back or said he's glad I'm feeling better these days. "The mouse is back," I say, finally breaking the silence in hopes of a conversation.

"Yeah?" he asks, not looking over at me.

"I got a new batch of peaches from the farm and put them on the table. Big mistake. Last night the little creep took a bite from each peach and then crapped in the bowl." I laugh, but Dad's quiet. He leans his head against his hand in deep thought.

"My old man could be a son-of-a-bitch."

"I thought you idolized him."

"I did. He was a damn good judge. Everyone respected him." He pauses and then barely audible, says, "He told me once how he found a mouse in the toilet. He set down paper for it so it could try to get out. But he didn't do it to help the poor son-a-bitch. He'd pull the paper out each time the mouse crawled up to the rim just to watch it fall back until it drowned."

"That's terrible and sick."

"Damn right it is," he mumbles. "I thought he was perfect." He flicks a mosquito away from his cheek. "And that horse face," he adds, referring to his mother. "Rotten son-of-a-bitch."

"Dad, she was your mother. Come on..."

"Don't give me that." He shakes his head. "She gave my old man bleeding ulcers. He died because she was a rotten son-of-a-bitch." I roll my eyes.

Here we go again. He's going to tell me how his mother nagged his father during dinner every night about his secretary (never mind the fact that he cheated on his wife for years.) About how she'd give my Dad castor oil and stare at him while he was on the toilet until he had a bowel movement. How hot it was at his father's funeral and how his mother forced him to wear white gloves and stockings under his knickers. And the long spiel about how she left him money in a trust fund that he wasn't allowed to access until he turned forty and by then, crooked lawyers in charge had dwindled it down to barely nothing. "She'd get all red in the face, and then I knew I had it coming," he says instead, startling me with this new information.

"What do you mean?"

"Every night, after my father died, she'd drink and get all red in the face and then go after me with her cane."

"Dad, you were only eleven. You didn't deserve that," I say, but he's out of reach. He stares into space without emotion.

Dad will probably never tell me any more than that, but I suspect there's a lot to tell. He keeps it well hidden like his bottles. And his love.

I still cook dinner for all of us, but Dad eats alone in the living room with the boob tube blaring and his plate balanced on his knees, and Mama and I eat together in the kitchen. Sometimes Dad gets a yen for Chinese, and he comes home and says, "Let's get some chinks" in his best Archie Bunker flare.

Tonight I made jasmine rice and curry shrimp, and Mama and I are at the table. We talk while Dad watches a wrestling match. "Don't waste your life," Mama says. "And don't ever end up like me, sixty two years old living in someone else's house and taking an old bitch's crap every day." Mama puts her fork down.

"Do the right thing. Care too much. Stand on our heads and bend over backwards. Take the blame. Be honest. Get kicked in the head with indifference. Live by the Golden Rule. Until one day you realize that sometimes 'drop dead' can save us," I announce with unapologetic cynicism.

"You're too young to be so bitter."

"Young," I repeat almost with disgust. "Don't remind

Prima Donna Sunshine

me, Mama." Truth is, I'm tired. Heart-tired and bone-tired.

"I want you to get your own life, Molly. Forget it. He's going down."

"I don't want you going down. That's all I care about right now."

"It's too late for me, Baby." She takes my hand with deep thought.

"What are you thinking?"

"After my Daddy died, my mother would wake me up in the middle of the night and ask me to take a walk with her. She'd carry a bottle in her coat, and we'd walk until four in the morning."

"How old were you?"

"Fourteen. She'd hand me the bottle, and I'd drink a little, too. When she got too drunk to walk, we'd sit on a curb until she sobered up a little, enough to walk back to the house." Mama chokes on tears. "And then my brothers Bobby and Alfred drank themselves to death before they were thirty-five. Little did I know that forty-eight years later Tom would be a worse drunk than all of them put together."

"I'm sorry, Mama."

"No, I'm sorry that I dragged you into our Hell."

"Leave him, Mama. Leave him here with The Old Bitch, the job, everything."

"I want to. I think about it every day. I just can't do it, Molly. It would be like putting a gun to his head."

"He's gonna die anyway!" I slam my hand on the table with exasperation.

"I can't leave him to die alone."

I decide to just change the subject. "How's the nosebleed?" I ask, referring to the nosebleed Dad has had now for three days.

"I've been trying to get that stubborn bastard to a doctor. He needs to get that nose packed."

"He'll have no choice if it gets bad enough."

"And The Old Bitch comes home tomorrow."

"Is she still talking about staying in New York more often and hiring that woman driver?"

"Yup. She wants her to stay with her at the penthouse a few days a week."

"What about Dad?"

"To help Dave with the grounds and the pool."

"Dave?"

"Yeah, a new guy, a groundskeeper."

"Dad not driving to New York and working at the estate. You know what that means."

"He'll be drunk twenty-four seven instead of taking care of the grounds." Mama buries her head in her hands. "What are we going to do? If The Old Bitch finds out about his boozing, we'll be on the street. Nowhere to go with a drunk."

"No, he'd be on the street, and you and I would start over somewhere."

"Sometimes I wish he'd just take a gun and kill all of us. It would be more humane."

"It's gonna be all right, Mama," I whisper. I lie through my teeth.

"I pray the angels will bring a miracle. They always have," she says with sudden revived faith when I hug her.

Perhaps she's lying through her teeth, too. Maybe it's to make herself feel better. Maybe it's a way to get through another day, like my dreams of flying out that window.

Prima Donna Sunshine

16

Dad's bombed more than ever, and Dave helps us remove his drunken ass out of The Old Bitch's sight when she comes home from New York. Minutes before she and her driver pull up the driveway in the Cadillac, Dad swings an arm around Dave's shoulder, and they shuffle past the indoor pool, through the solarium and out the back door. Dave gets him into our Jeep, and then I take him home. Each time Dave bails out my Dad I can barely look him in the eye because I'm so embarrassed.

Dave's a sweet, soft-spoken man with an easy smile and ready humor, even when "I love ya, Buthdy," is a slurred mantra all the way to the car, and Dad's weight almost pulls Dave down with him.

Christmas will be here soon, and I'm on strike for the first time in my life. I don't care if Zane and Linda are coming Christmas Eve, if the house is decorated or even in order.

In fact, I am so cynical about this whole family holiday fantasy that I am making a farce of it.

Every year until now, Dad had cut down or bought us a fir, and I would do the rest. Since Dad's too drunk this year, I take matters into my own hands. I decide to cut down a skinny one from our back yard.

I go out with a saw and slice it down in a fit while I talk to myself. "I'll give them all a holiday," I mumble. "Molly the lumberjack dyke at your service." I feel our old neighbor The Stick watching me from her window. "Yes, it's official. We're all nuts over here!" I say, hoping she can hear me.

I stomp back into the house, jam the white pine into a tree stand and watch it fall to one side. "Perfect. The tree looks drunk. A drunken tree for a drunk," I say out loud as I fetch anything to stuff up the space so it will stand straighter. No luck. I place it in the corner between the windows, tie a string around its trunk and then tack the string into the wall. I dust off my hands and put on some tiny white lights, a couple of ornaments, and then stand back and cry.

It's pathetic. Sadder than Charlie Brown's. A poor tree that was trying so hard to grow strong and tall was murdered and tied to a corner of a crazy house so Molly Dorman could prove how pissed off she is.

Mama bursts out laughing when she comes home and sees it. "Hey, it's a tree. Now we can get Christmas over with," I say.

"Molly, my poor girl," she says, stifling her laugh as she puts a soft hand to my cheek. "Come on. Let's make the best of it. It might be your father's last Christmas." Her words are like a dart through my cynicism. "Let's get a real tree. Maybe we can make decorations from this poor thing," she adds.

And that's what we do. While Dad sleeps one off, we go to a Christmas tree farm on one of the back roads and pick out a white fir, one with blue-gray needles that smell like oranges when they're crushed between our fingers.

A cold wind scatters miniscule stars of snow against the windshield on our way home, and Mama puts on the radio to hear Christmas carols. "Come on, the hell with him. We'll have a good holiday, Baby," she says cheerfully. She sings along to *Silver Bells* and smacks my knee until I smile with great reluctance. "How many pie orders do you have?" she asks between stanzas.

"Too many," I whine. "I don't know what possessed me to bake pies for the health food store. I'll be peeling apples and pumpkins until after New Year's."

"Speaking of, I can't wait to see this year end." Mama slows down when the light kiss of snow turns into a squall. It whites out the road. "So long 1991. Don't let the door hit you in the ass on the way out." I laugh in spite of everything.

"Hey, I heard Neil Diamond will be coming to New York next summer," I say.

"You're driving into the city with that clunker?" she

asks, referring to Blue Eyes whose mileage is in dog years.

"I'm going by space ship if I have to." We both laugh.

Two miles down the road the snow comes to an abrupt halt, and sunlight clears any accumulation on the road like an eraser on a blackboard.

"Life is like that snow squall, Baby. Things can change in a blink of an eye."

Dad's at the Bosco's cleaning the pool, and I'm home in the kitchen baking pies while Mama and Joni, my Mom's show business friend, catch up over tea. Joni is filling her in on the latest news about her singing group and their recent gig in Atlantic City. "I saw Tom again at the liquor store," she adds casually, slipping it in as a bye and bye. That's funny. Last night, Dad said the same thing about her.

I press pie crusts together with a fork while I restrain a sarcastic comment. It amazes me how some people can have their hand in the cookie jar and talk about someone else's hand in the cookie jar.

Yes, Joni drinks. Sometimes she calls Mama at night and slurs her words with show biz flare. The drunker she is, the more colorful she is. It's almost charming, until she comes out with a jab about Mama's music. Mama just shakes her head and avoids calling her in the evenings.

I guess booze gives some people the nerve to say and do what they wouldn't dream of sober. I'd hate to think what would come out of my mouth if I ever got drunk.

Maybe someday I'll get over my distaste for the stuff and see what happens.

I'm on my nineteenth pie. Six more to go. All homemade, organic, and wrapped with holiday pretty. It's become a sort of meditation, peeling and slicing until my hands go a little numb. The scents of holiday spices in this house are worth the hard work, though I'm sure the profit won't be.

I'm an odd duck at twenty-two. Every other twenty-something someone I know, including Fred, parties hard. Fred has this notion that getting drunk is a social accomplishment, maybe artsy and glamorous. I'd like to show him a scrapbook from the past six years in my father's life including morning shakes, bleeding uncontrollably from the nose and ass, getting a third-world bloated belly, shitting his pants because he couldn't make it to the toilet, and shrinking so many brain cells that he can no longer hold a mundane conversation. Yeah, drinking rocks.

I stick four more pies in the oven and think about my manuscript that is now sitting on my desk gathering dust. I've tried to write again, to conjure words and feel the pen move sometimes almost without me. Whatever it is, I've lost it.

I submitted some work to a local magazine, and they plan on publishing a poem or two in the near future. They only pay twenty-five dollars, but it's something.

I notice that I don't do simple things anymore, things that once made me happy, as if joy is something to be postponed until circumstances are different. Like noticing the sun set or looking at the stars. Even my prayer altar is a catch-all for books and clutter. The heavens—and heaven—are insignificant.

Rob used to say that life is a spiritual journey, and the path is known to test us. He never said there would be no path.

I think of Rob often and wish I could see the blue shimmer in his eyes, for his hands on my body one more time. The Old Bitch says that she never hears from him and that he's probably found enlightenment in that ashram in India. Zane always says to find happiness and to keep it a secret. I like to think that is what Rob is doing.

Last night I dreamed of a woman. She came to me wearing a black suede jacket with fringes, and she was my lover. I know it was only a dream, but she said I was beautiful, and I woke up crying.

I want to fly out of this house and this God-forsaken town. I want to be on a beach where there is youth and music and poetry in the waves.

I want to ride a lover's rapids on a bed white with sun. I dream of women and men who are mine, of swallowing heaven whole. I dream of becoming a river—a river of white-water lovers—my soul wide open, without form, only a body of tears.

Mama and I put up the tree and decorated it with Victorian flare including framed family photographs. I forced myself out of Scrooge mode and wove garlands from oranges, apples, and the poor pine I had chopped down in a fit. I made a feast of spiced leg of lamb. Zane and Linda came over on Christmas Eve bearing an abundance of food--tiger shrimp, cookies and cakes, and a box of canned delights from their garden.

The Old Bitch had planned on staying in New York until the holidays were over. It was the first Christmas in ten years that my parents didn't have to be at the Boscos. Dad came down with an ear infection that left him temporarily stone deaf in his good ear, and we all resorted to exasperated sign language to communicate with him. Of course Zane's version was nothing less than slapstick humor that left all of us in stitches.

Dad was half-sober, and for the most part, everything was perfect. Too perfect, like the sinister calm before a record storm.

17

January came in with Dad going on binges for days at a time. Mama told The Old Bitch he was sick, some sort of reoccurring flu. The Old Bitch took it surprisingly well then later decided to take it out on Mama by screaming at her for hours about her so-called incompetence. Mama, passive as usual, swallowed all of it and tried to tune her out, anything to keep the roof over our heads, mainly my father's drunken head.

I've had to cancel my art classes indefinitely. "Oh, Molly, I hope nothing's wrong," a concerned mother said to me on the phone.

"My Dad's sick," I said, choking back tears. Yeah, sick in the head but no sicker than Mama and me.

Right now Dad's in bed drunk as a skunk and calling out The Old Bitch's name, "Rosa..." He sounds like a moose in rutting season.

Prima Donna Sunshine

"What did you say, Tom?" Mama asks as she passes their bedroom on the way into the kitchen.

"Rosa...whah a pair of friggin' legs."

"You son-of-a-bitch," Mama says as she turns around on a dime.

"What beauthiful tits."

"You're in love with that old bitch!"

"Fug you, Emma..."

"She's made our lives Hell for ten years, you bastard."

I'm in the living room finishing up a sketch, and I get up and watch from the bedroom doorway.

"Drop dead. Leaver alone. Rosa, what a piece..." Mama goes nuts and slaps him in the face. She grabs a pillow and belts him with it until Dad tries to shield his face with his fists. "Crazy sunnava bitch!"

"You can have that bandy-legged old bitch. You always fell for whores. I wasted my life on you, you drunken bastard!"

"Go fug yursel and that worthless daughter of yurs."

"I'm gonna kill you, Tom. Say it one more time, and I'll kill you!" Mama stands over him again.

"Worthless!" And that's when Mama blows like Vesuvius. She jumps on the bed and straddles him so he can't move. She slaps him like King Kong swatting planes.

"Mama!" I yell, crying and trying not to laugh simultaneously.

"Hel, help! She's gun-na kill me! Call the cops, Molly!" he yells, putting his hands up like a punch-drunk fighter with blurred vision.

"Don't think I wouldn't," Mama says, finally rolling to the other side of the bed.

"Yur fuggin crazy...fuggin crazy," he says over and over until he falls to sleep.

Mama just lies there and starts laughing. A chuckle then a deep belly laugh before she sobs uncontrollably.

Dad has decided to just lie down and die. He no longer gets dressed, refuses to go to work, and stays in bed with a bottle under the mattress from morning until night. When he empties the bottle or we pour it down the drain, he fetches another one from his hidden collection somewhere in the house.

Mama told The Old Bitch that Dad is still sick and needs some time off. That was two months ago, and he's still in bed. It's winter and the Bosco grounds don't need much work, and that's the only thing in Dad's favor.

Mama goes to work, and I am under house arrest keeping him alive by hiding his booze and trying to make him eat. He only takes a few sips of broth and then shoves the bowl away.

Sometimes he forgets where he hides his stash. He stumbles out of bed naked with the intention of getting in the car to drive. He threatens to walk to the liquor store when we hide the car keys. Two times he staggered as far as the garage and then fell onto the cold cement.

Mama says he'll go into serious detox without booze and could die at this point, so until we find him help, we're giving him watered-down vodka like a baby who needs a bottle. Even half out of his mind he knows there's water in it, and he screams for more especially in the middle of the night.

Mama moved out of the bedroom and onto the hard-ass living room couch. Nobody gets any sleep with him yelling for more booze, not even Schnapps.

Mama, without sleep, gets up at six to go to work and spends every waking moment trying to get Dad to a hospital rehab. Every facility from here to California says the same thing: he has to go to rehab on his own volition.

Mama ends up in tears and screaming to the person on the other end that it's too late for him to make that decision for himself, that he doesn't even get up to go to the bathroom anymore and pisses the bed.

Mama comes home around seven-thirty at night, and we both turn him over just enough to be able to change the sheets. "Tom!" she screams at him. "You've gotta get help! You're dying!"

"Fug you," he says over and over in his stupor. "Fug 'em all."

Last night I dreamed of a blond woman on the beach. Her white shawl billowed in the wind, and her gold hair was gathered in a Victorian bun. The platinum sea was a burning galaxy in the morning light. The woman didn't bend to pick up shells or walk at the water's edge with a lover.

She drowned herself.

Today, she is on my easel, and her hair is blowing like

gold dust in the wind. Her back is to me, and I paint a sense of peace that I can hardly grasp. This painting is my last link to questionable sanity.

Like Mama, I can barely function. The house has gone to ruin. I can't muster the incentive to clean or cook. I open cans of soup and try to eat.

The Christmas tree is still up, standing in the corner of the living room like a dead body. There is a two inch pile of dried needles at its base, and our family pictures fall off one at a time into the heap. We have all officially gone crazy.

Dad yells hour upon hour from the bedroom as I blend pastels and go into the eye of the storm. "Come here you worthless cunt!" His words feel like hurricane winds bludgeoning the sea cliff of my resistance. I remain suspended in the blond woman's world, feel the sun on my back, inhale salt wind, but even the strongest cliffs wear down with enough force. "Hey Worthless!" he blows again. I continue painting, tears burning down my face. "Molly! Molly! Get me a drink! Molly!"

I've grown to despise my name.

I sign my painting, stomp to the kitchen and grab a vodka bottle. This time I don't water it down. I throw it near him onto the bed. "Go on, kill yourself with it and leave me out of it!" I yell.

"Ah, thanks...thank God, Molly," he says softly as his hands search the bed blindly for the bottle. "Worthless bitch," he mumbles as his fingers finally grasp it. He spills some of it as he pours it into his mouth. "Help me, please..." He starts crying because he keeps missing his lips. I walk out of the room. "You rotten little bastard, get over here!"

But I'm out of reach. Finished, shut down. Imploding.

18

Mama, desperate to get help for Dad, broke down and told The Old Bitch everything. Shockingly, she took my mother into her arms and then picked up the phone and let her money talk. Within a half hour, The Old Bitch had a family counselor and cutting-edge rehab facility on the phone. Within two hours, there was a room waiting for Dad and an expert panel of professionals.

All we have to do is get him to go.

"Fuck you, fuck all of you bastards. I ain't going anywhere," he says surprisingly coherent between watered-down hits.

"Tom, you've gotta go. You're dying, and we're dying with you."

"I'll die right here before I go to any fucking rehab. There's nothing wrong with me. I can stop any time I want to."

"Tommy, you need help, Honey," Mama cries.

"Dad, you can't stop on your own. You're in a medical crisis now. You need help, and we have it for you. Please!" I start wailing.

"Go to Hell. I'll die first, you son-of-a-bitches," he says, reaching for another sip from the bottle under his pillow. Mama and I stare at him.

"Tom, do it for your kid."

"Fuck the kid," he says flatly. "Worthless bitch."

"Tom, you put a knife in my heart," Mama says, crying out of control. "Please! I'll do anything…I'll give you your freedom. You can even have that Old Bitch if she wants you when you sober up. Just get help! I beg you, on my knees." Mama kneels down by the side of the bed and takes his face in her hands. "Tommy, please, please!"

"Get outta here! Leave me alone. Go fuck yourselves and tell Rosa, 'thanks a lot'." He stares at the ceiling and shakes his head in disbelief. "I can't believe it. Her, too." Mama sobs into the mattress. Dad is oblivious.

"You think that's all I'm good for, working my ass off for both of us and then coming home to change your diaper?" Mama screams. "Would you do that for me, you son-of-a-bitch?"

"Drop dead, Emma," he says and then goes into another rant for more booze, full strength, or he's going to walk to the liquor store. In his shit-filled diaper.

Mama and I haven't slept in days. It's the third night without even a full hour's rest. Dad's in one of his nocturnal rants. "Emma! Emma!" he screams from the bedroom just as we start to doze off. It goes on hour upon hour. Mama gets up at least four times to shut him up, but it's no use.

"Hey Worthless!" he's yelling right now. "Where's that worthless motherfugger?" I shift in bed, bury myself under blankets, but nothing drowns it out. "Hey Worthless!"

I feel the walls close in on me. I feel like a miner trapped underground, and the air is running out. I take deep breaths, close the pillow tighter around my ears. I hear the blood in my ears coming in like a violent tide, but nothing turns off the sound coming from that bedroom where the Devil screams, "Hey Worthless!"

Trance-like, I get out of bed and head down the hallway. I hear a voice. My voice. "I'm gonna kill him. It ends right here, right now."

"Molly..." Mama says from the living room. She's so weak that her words are barely audible.

"Hey Worthless!" The Devil says again. I continue down the hallway half out of my mind and half out of my body. I feel as if I'm walking beside myself—watching, listening—but trapped behind glass.

"I'm gonna kill him, smash his brains in. We can say he got up, fell, and hit his head. Case closed," I announce. The air around me feels sharp, a tunnel of knives.

Something pulls at me from behind, and I realize it's Mama, grabbing my nightgown with all her strength. "Baby, it's not worth it! You don't know what you're saying!" she yells to get my attention, but I continue down the hall like a programmed assassin on a mission. She pulls harder and strangles my neck with my nightgown before it almost rips. We wrestle against the wall.

"I wanna kill him!" I finally scream so loud that I slam back in my body. "I'm gonna kill him! One blow to the head, and it's over!!" I scream, choking on tears so violent I feel my gut turn inside out. "I can't take anymore! I can't take anymore, Mama! I can't take anymore!" I say over and over until I almost puke. I pry myself out of her grip and make my way into the bedroom.

"There's Worthless," Dad says when I flick on the light by punching the switch. The room smells like old piss. I grab the wooden cane by the bed and swirl it in my hands to find the best grip for the job.

"Molly!!" Mama screams and barrels toward me before I can lift it over his head.

"Waz goin' on?" he asks, dead to the world with his thick tongue half out of his filthy mouth.

"If I don't kill him, I'm gonna kill myself!" I scream again, melting down until my knees buckle.

"Where's that worless bitch... go get yur bitch," he slurs, staring at the ceiling light over the bed. Mama turns to look at him and jumps on top of him without warning. Whatever demon was in my body is now in hers, and Mama starts punching Dad without pause. In the face, the arm, the chest.

"I dare you to say that to my kid one more time, you drunken animal," she says between gritted teeth.

"Get off me, you crazy bitch," Dad says as he flails his

arms and tries to swing at her.

"Mama, stop it!" I yell, grabbing her by her sweatshirt the same way she grabbed me in the hallway. She runs out of strength.

"Oh, God, they're fuggin' crazy mullerfuggers," Dad says with his eyes wide open. He slams his arms on either side of the bed and tries to get up, but he's helpless as a beetle on his back. "I gotta get outta here. I'm gon-na get a furnished room, you crazy bathstards."

I stumble back to bed with shaking legs. Mama soon follows, and I hear her settle back onto the couch in the other room, sobbing into a pillow. I pray Dad curses himself to sleep so we can doze off. "I'm sorry my precious child. I love you, Baby. Don't go crazy," Mama cries in the other room. "I need you."

When I was five, Dad and I went out for the afternoon, and my thumb got caught in the car door when he closed it. I screamed bloody murder as my finger puffed up and throbbed in steady beats. "Why'd you hurt me?" I asked him as my tears soaked his shirt. He got a cup of ice from a nearby luncheonette and stuck my finger in it as quickly as possible. I looked up at him once the pain started to subside and saw him crying right along with me.

"I'd never hurt you on purpose. You're Daddy's little girl," he said, and I reached my good hand out to his cheek to dry his face.

I'm at the hospital on this March eighteenth waiting for

Dad to become conscious. After so many weeks without nourishment and this past week without fluids, he got too sick to fight medical help. Two days ago Mama and Dave were finally able to get him to the hospital.

I stand in the doorway of his hospital room and remember that day when I was a little girl. It's easier for me to remember days like that now that Dad's silent and small. He's hooked up to machines, his face an ashen three-quarter moon. The doctors say he has double pneumonia, internal bleeding, and severe dehydration. They say there is a good chance that he won't make it.

I am not yet able to sit by him. He is a fragile stranger in that bed, and we are meeting for the first time in years. Aside from those few months in 1989 when he had lost his license, it's the first time in a decade that I've seen him completely sober.

There is a man here named Gabriel, and he's been assigned to Dad if he pulls through. He is a counselor and a recovering alcoholic. "Your father seems strong," he tells me with a smile. "Don't give up on him."

"What makes you so sure?" I ask.

"Been there," he says with a confidence.

"If only we could have gotten him help before he got so sick," Mama says, crying.

"Mrs. Dorman, I'm afraid that's how the system works. There is no help until an alcoholic wants help. Some have to almost die, and unfortunately, some do."

"How can a person out of their mind make a decision like that when they don't even know what day it is?"

"I understand your frustration, Mrs. Dorman. But it has has taken years for your husband to get to this stage. It's easy to make it easy for someone because you love them."

"It's more complicated than that, Gabriel."

"That's why they call it co-dependency." He smiles and touches her hand. "Don't beat yourselves up. We do what we think we should in the moment." He pauses to make a notation on his clipboard. "I'll check back tomorrow," he says.

"Thanks, Gabriel," Mama says, and I follow suit.

"Call me Gabe." He puts his pen in his suit pocket and then leaves.

Mama goes to the cafeteria to get a bite to eat, and I take her seat by Dad's bed. The fluorescent light over his head makes him look like a figure in a wax museum. He looks more dead than alive as a slideshow of memories flash in my brain, glimpses of the man he once was beneath the rubble.

I see him picking wild roses with me when I was five; his big hands bending a stem while he shows me how to trespass the thorns. The scent of cotton candy-pink petals, his laugh when he gives me a bloom to sniff and the yellow tuft in the center tickles my nose.

I see him on his day off, and he smells like hard work and cut grass. A ghost moon rises out of the twilight while the melancholy call of the whippoorwill pierces the gloaming. Dad and I are out on the deck of our mountain home. We watch bats fly in staccato, and darkness bleeds into the twilight like fresh watercolor on thirsty paper. I'm subtle as a rock breaking the glass of a still pond when I barrel into Dad's lap and demand access to his thoughts. He ignores my inquiry and points out the Big Dipper and the whippoorwill on the wire. "In this world, you learn more by listening than by talking," he says, motioning for me to glance up at the diamond expanse over our heads.

Memories shift. I'm walking with Dad to pick up litter on the unpaved back roads near our house. "Slobs!" he exclaims as he bends down with frustration to pick up yet another soda can along the wayside. He moves in quiet grace even while walking on the ball of his foot because of his frozen knee; through the forest's thickest undergrowth, Dad advances almost without sound, barely snapping a twig. He pauses. We stand still, and I wonder what's holding Dad's attention. A sun-faceted leaf drifts down in adagio time amid the fiddlehead ferns. "I feel Indians here," he whispers. I peer into the shadows and expect to see ancient faces appear within the dappled tapestry.

I see him playing tennis with me when I was thirteen. I have the worst back hand in town yet he chases after that ball with his bad leg so many times that any other father would advise me to just hang up my racket. But he keeps playing, and I keep apologizing when he hobbles after the ball without complaint.

I see him driving an hour away to pick up tickets to my first Neil Diamond concert and letting out ear-shattering whistles during the finale just to let me know how sorry he is that he was jealous of my crush on a singer and that he really does like his music.

I also see how he starts to ignore me and withhold affection. Little by little, the names for me under his breath, barely audible behind my back. Lard ass. Prima Donna. Worthless. The fucking kid.

The years I tried to be visible, ways I devise to be seen. Cooking. Keeping house. Crying. Screaming.

I see myself standing over him with a wooden cane just a few weeks ago, intent on bludgeoning the life out of him.

I wanted to kill my own father, I say out loud to myself as I watch him take labored breaths that sound like he's drowning. *I'm so sorry, Dad. Please forgive me. God forgive me. Please live. I forgive you for everything, just live.*

19

It is almost two weeks later, and Dad's making a turn for the better. Mama and I go to the hospital each day and sometimes bring him some fresh vegetable juice in a jar and leave it by his bedside. He woke up for a little while today before falling back to sleep. He smiled at me before he dozed off, the sweet smile I never thought I'd see again.

Gabriel comes in and immediately zeros in on the jar of juice by the bed. "What's this?" he asks with knitted brows.

"Vegetable juice."

"From where?"

"I squeezed it before we came. He needs the nutrients."

"I have to report this," he announces as he grabs the jar with obvious agitation. "This happens all the time. Families pray for their loved one's sobriety then sneak them alcohol."

"What?" I yell. Mama motions for me to shut up, but I can't. "Are you out of your mind?" I have a sudden urge to pluck every hair out of this guy's overgrown mustache and then kick him where the sun don't shine.

"Gabe, we tried to move heaven and earth to get him help. Why on earth would we jeopardize his recovery?" Mama asks calmly.

"I'm sorry, but I have to take this and have it analyzed," he says as he leaves the room in a fit of annoyance.

"I don't believe this," I say, kicking the wall.

"Molly, ssh!" Mama hisses at me as if I'm a toddler.

"How can you sit there and get accused of something as insane as this?"

"Because he's the only one that can help him, Molly. And besides, the bastard won't find anything in that juice."

Of course he doesn't. Two days later he comes into Dad's room, pulls us aside, and apologizes sheepishly. "I'm sorry. I was out of line."

"Over the top out of line," I remind him. Gabe looks down and shuffles the sole of his shoe against the floor. He looks nervous and guilty.

"I was jealous."

"What?" Mama asks.

"When I was at death's door, I didn't have a family to rally around me. I think I was just jealous, plain and simple. I'm sorry. Let's leave it at that." He heads for the door and turns around halfway, avoiding our eyes. "I'm glad to see him taking a turn for the better." Mama and I look at each other with disbelief.

An hour later the doctor informs us that aside from his weakened state, Dad most likely has permanent brain damage and will need to be in a nursing home for the rest of his life. "I'm sorry, I don't believe that," Mama says outright.

"It's my professional opinion, Mrs. Dorman," he says. "We will make arrangements."

Dad wakes up and mumbles something. We go over to him and pat his shoulders. "Tommy, we're here," Mama says, caressing his cheek that needs a shave.

"Emma, come here," he whispers. Mama leans over. "I need a drink."

"Tommy, you're never drinking again."

"No, you don't understand. I need a drink. I need a drink." His rolls his eyes as if he's trying to focus. "Where am I?"

"You're in the hospital."

"What the fuck for?"

"You almost died."

"Never mind that. Give me a drink." I lean my head on the bed railing.

"Do you believe this?" Mama asks me.

"Hell yeah," I say, looking up. "Hell yeah."

I was desperate for a change of scene, away from

hospitals and Dad's snail-pace recovery. Zane and I attended the anniversary celebration of Walt Whitman's life in Camden, New Jersey. They unveiled a statue of the poet with a butterfly poised on his forefinger, and a performer wove in and out of the crowd as he recited Whitman's most poignant works.

Zane is feeling better, on the verge of remission and talks about "going down the road." It's the expression he most often uses when he isn't getting enough attention and wants to get in his car and keep driving.

By the time we pull into our driveway, a cold April rain splashes the windshield of his Ford, and he's in a mood. We sit in his truck waiting for the downpour to dwindle. "Look, I don't know how long I'm going to be around. I don't know what that means to you, but to me it means that time is precious. I want to see you more often, and I don't want to hear your list of excuses."

"Zane, I know time is precious. And there are reasons, not excuses, why I haven't seen you these past couple months." My heart's pounding already from adrenaline.

"Let me tell you something. Tom will live because he's selfish. I'm your flesh and blood, and you owe me some of the same compassion you give him," he says. His face tightens like a mask.

"I'm doing the best I can right now, Zane. Please, I can't take any more pressure."

"I'm your father, not Tom! I'm dying, God dammit and that's something you think you don't have time for!" His face turns purple, and he slams his hand on the steering wheel.

"Please don't put me in the middle of both of you," I plead.

"It's either him or me! You owe me, God dammit!"

"I owe you nothing!" I scream.

"After everything I've done for you!"

"Send me a bill," I spit.

"I'll cut you out. You won't get one painting after I die."

"No one emotionally blackmails me. Don't even go there."

"*I'm* your father!"

"That man you call selfish is the only father I'll ever call a father. No matter what, he's earned that. And if you think you're gonna do to me what you did to my mother, you're dead wrong." I grab my bag and open the passenger door.

"I'll burn those fucking paintings before I leave them to you! You're out!"

"You can take your paintings and shove them up your ass!"

"Go to Hell!" he screams, his words reverberating inside the car like trapped lightning.

"Fuck you!" I scuffle out of the truck, dropping my bag on the ground.

"Die!" he bellows through the glass, and I kick his car door. I go in for another slam, intent on denting it like the Incredible Hulk as he starts the engine. He slams the truck into reverse, and his tires screech against the pavement as he flies out of the driveway. I'm shaking so hard I can barely walk into the house.

I never want to see him again.

Dad has been moved to a nursing home in Morristown while he gets his strength back. And his marbles.

Mama has complete faith that his disorientation and memory lapses are temporary. I don't know what to think.

Before Dad left the hospital, Gabe talked to him on a few occasions, but nothing penetrated his brain. "He's too far gone," Gabe announced coldly. "I can't do anything with him in his condition."

Alcohol hasn't touched Dad's lips in over a month, but he still has a one-track mind. "Did you bring what I asked for?" he asks Mama and me the minute we walk into his room.

"I don't want to hear it, Tom," Mama says.

"Come on, you're kidding. You wouldn't let me down, not my Emma," he says as he sits in a wheelchair and fiddles endlessly with the hem of his hospital gown.

"Tom, we drove almost an hour to see you. Stop talking about booze," Mama says.

"You've got it inside your boot, don't you? You put a bottle in your boot," he decides cheerfully and gives me a wink. I look down at my knee-high black suede boots and shake my head.

"Gee, that would be a good way to sneak it in," I say.

"Oh, come on, I know you have it."

"Dad, I don't have any booze on me. Forget it." I flop

into the chair by the window and wonder if he read the letter I gave him during my last visit. There have been so many things I wanted to tell him since his brush with death, so many things now that he's not drunk, but I can't conjure a single sentence when we're face to face. It's easier to put it on paper.

I notice that my letter has been opened, and it's stuck inside the copy of Walt Whitman's *Specimen Days* that I also left for him.

"Did you read Molly's letter?" Mama asks him as she sits on his bed.

"Emma, don't get me mad. I asked you to get me something, *you know.*" He winks again.

"Tom, your kid wrote you a letter. Did you read the damn thing or not?" Mama's running out of patience.

"Yeah, yeah, for chrissake. Never mind that!" He swats his hand in front of his face with exaggerated annoyance.

"Tom, that letter was important to Molly," Mama persists, but I know it's useless. He launches into mindless chatter with Mama as I stare out the window.

A haze of spring hovers over the wet April landscape. I amuse myself by thinking about how Mama and I finally mustered enough energy and motivation to finally take down that Christmas tree carcass. It took over an hour to suck up the mound of dead needles.

I try to escape by looking out the window, but I can't stop tears burning my eyes.

I told him in the letter how much I still love him and how I believe in his recovery and sobriety. I told him how proud I am of him for all that he had done right through the years and that I'd be there for him when he gets back home. I apologized for not being a better daughter.

All he can do is swat his hands in annoyance, gibbering about nonsense. He also claims that he's being abused by one of the aides. "Emma, listen to me. You've gotta get me outta here. He's a crazy son-of-bitch. He comes in every morning and roughs me up when he's getting me out of bed," he says with vehemence. I roll my eyes. I simply don't believe it. I've heard about this sort of thing in nursing homes, but I'm so pissed off that even if it is true, I get a vicarious thrill knowing that someone is smacking the shit out of him.

"Come on, take me for a ride, and I'll get it," Dad says to Mama.

"Get what?"

"You know...ssh!" He puts his index finger to his lips.

"Tom, I can't take you out anywhere. You're stuck here until you get better. And you're never seeing another drop of booze as long as you live."

"Please, Emma! You're a cold son-of-a-bitch. You and that kid over there."

"That's it," Mama says suddenly. She grabs her purse. "Come on, Molly. Let's get out of here. Bye, Tom," Mama says, waving.

"Where are ya goin'?" he asks.

"Home," I say.

"All you care about is booze. We're leaving," Mama adds, but he thinks she means something else.

"Now you're talkin'. You're goin' home to get me some, aren't you? Don't be too long," he says. "I'll sit in this chair and wait for you to come back. I'm thirsty, Emma. Don't be too damn long."

The Old Bitch is on the war path since Dad refused treatment. She's decided that Mama is worth keeping, and she's come up with a plan to sell our house and have us move into the Bosco guest cabin. "Emma, it's time you and Tom get out of that house. It's ridiculous you're not living here on the premises. And besides, it would save me money. I need every dime," she told Mama three weeks ago. "You can move into the guest cabin. Yes, that's what we'll do." And without another word, our house went on the market.

Yeah, Mrs. B needs the money. And my imaginary lesbian lover knocked me up.

She also told Mama, "If Tom dies it will be just the two of us. Won't that be nice, Emma? Who needs men? Who needs the old bastards? You'll take care of me, won't you, Emma? You and Molly?"

I don't know how Mama and I are going to empty out nine years of living in this house single-handedly. Dave offered to help us with the big pieces, namely that God-forsaken king size bed my parents inherited when they took the job and moved into the house. The moron before them apparently built it in the bedroom from scratch with no intentions of ever dismantling it. Dave has plans to come over with a hack saw and take it out piece by piece like a dismembered body.

I miss my classes and my kids. The mother of one of the girls offered to hold classes at her house after they finish their renovations. We'll see. In the meantime, I'm still working for the Donahues and giving Gracie private lessons once a week at their house.

Zane called Mama tonight and told her that I'm a no-good ingrate. He also said, "She's a bad seed, Emma. There's something wrong with that girl!" He was screaming so loud that I could hear every syllable boiling over the receiver when Mama held it away from her ear.

"That daughter of ours has a heart you will never begin to know," she said, holding back tears. When Zane realized she wasn't siding with him, he called her every name in the book. I grabbed the phone out of her hands.

"No one talks to my mother like that, you hear me, Zane Davis? Go straight to Hell!"

"She used me! I was just a stud to sire the likes of *you*!" he bellowed in my ear like he was gargling nails. I slammed down the phone so hard that I cracked the receiver.

"We need a new one anyway," Mama said. And then we started laughing. There was nothing left to do.

21

Over the course of the week, I've done twelve loads of laundry, packed forty boxes, and prayed for sanity. When Mama isn't packing, she and Dave take anything to the dump that's too old or too cumbersome. A lot will be going into storage, including Mama's beloved piano. The cabin is already furnished and just too small. I know her heart is broken.

Dave has also been organizing the garage while we sort through closets. We've all found so many hidden bottles of booze that we shout with sarcastic glee with each new discovery.

Dad was released from the nursing home a few days ago after tests revealed that he's recovered his mental capacity. The doctor shook his head because he couldn't find an explanation for it. Mama, thank heavens, was right about that one.

Prima Donna Sunshine

Dad's physical strength is improving, but he's relying on that wheel chair like a kid with a security blanket. Schnapps is scared of it but attempts to sniff the spinning wheels until he gets too close and Dad yells, "Get outta here, you black bastard!"

I've waited eight years for Dad to be without a bottle, but I think I liked him better when he was sloshed. He's nastier than ever, critical of everything and everyone, and guzzles seltzer all day long. Half deaf or not, he can somehow hear an ant fart. His nerves are so on edge that if one of us sets a spoon down on the counter he bellows about the noise in the house.

Easter came and went, and I painted Dad a special card celebrating his homecoming. He set it aside like the letter I had written him a couple weeks ago and then asked for a cup of coffee. He's sober, but not much has changed.

Little by little, I've been bringing some of my things over to the Bosco cabin. Mama and Dad will be living upstairs, and I'll be downstairs in the studio apartment. I look forward to having some sort of privacy. It's not enough room to have art classes, but I'm content with its fully-equipped kitchen, driftwood dining table, full living room set, and private bathroom with a washer and dryer. I even have a private entrance in case I get some moxie and want to sneak in a lover.

There are no windows, and my easel is too tall to stand anywhere without hitting the ceiling, so to my dismay, I'll be painting upstairs or outside on the porch.

Our new driveway faces the Bosco's neighbor, the artist

I've heard about through the years. From my nosey observation through the cedars, he's married and has four kids and three dogs, and he stomps his feet as he chases one of them outside whenever they get too noisy. I've only caught blurred glimpses of him, but I'm hoping that he's gorgeous and has an open marriage.

I'm holding tickets to Neil Diamond's August sixteenth show at Madison Square Garden. Even though it's three months away, I'm already giddy with expectation. I may be a grown woman, but I plan on screaming with all the other grown women, so loud that I lose my voice just like I did when I was thirteen and I was hoarse for a week.

Good 'ole Neil. Maybe someday he'll realize that I'm his soul mate after all; maybe when I'm seventy-one and he's ninety-nine we'll finally meet, and we'll have a half hour together.

Yes, I'm crazy. Fred says that I remind him of a hare-brained squirrel. He says it with affection, but of course, I take it personally. I take everything personally. I think it's my fault when the sun doesn't shine.

Yesterday the movers transported our belongings to the cabin. The Old Bitch had Mama take care of her nonsense even though she knew that the movers were on their way. Dad, still confined to the wheel chair, watched the chaos with a nasty expression. The moving truck got stuck in a patch of mud around a corner and spun its wheels for twenty minutes, and somebody cracked my easel on the way into the house. I had to go to the bathroom like there was no tomorrow. I held out long as I could and helped direct clueless guys with boxes.

While I was in the bathroom, I could hear Dad cursing me out upstairs, "God damn worthless lard bitch." If I wasn't constipated as an old lady after a bowl of wet cement, I would have choked him.

Mom arrived fifteen minutes before the movers left, and I finally resurfaced. "God-damned worthless kid," he said one more time. After the commotion, Dave popped in to see if he could help us unpack. Dad was all piss and vinegar, and Mama and Dave stepped outside so they could talk without the soundtrack of profanity. "Worthless lard ass," he mumbled under his breath, this time referring to Dave.

Mama came back into the cabin a few minutes later and heard Dad's, uh, appreciation. "I don't know where we'd be without that man. He's a gift from God, and you better know it!" she yelled.

"He's a worthless son-of-a-bitch. We don't need him," he declared and then started crying like a baby because he can't get out of that "god-damned chair" and "be a man."

Speaking of that God-damned chair, the wheels on the upstairs floor reverberate through my ceiling and sound like an anaconda slithering inside the walls. I catch myself lying in bed and grinding my teeth whenever I hear it. I may have forgiven Dad for mostly everything, but I still resent him as much as I love him, and it's even harder to forgive myself.

Prima Donna Sunshine

A full moon glistens like a burnt opal over the lake as Fred and I lean against my car and listen to the fields humming with summer crickets. The air is earthy and sweet from rolls of hay that dot the dusky landscape. "I don't know," he answers when I ask him what he dreams about.

"Come on, you must have something you'd like to do after your second stint in the Service."

"I guess I'd like to own a book store, be surrounded by books."

"Sounds like a good dream." I scuff my foot on pebbles that glint silver in the twilight.

"You?" Fred asks, folding his arms across his chest. I can tell he's showing off his developed biceps like a proud peacock.

"I want to write."

"I thought you already do."

"I mean actually finish something. See it published with my name on it."

"So what's stopping you?"

"Me." I sigh with frustration and stretch my back against the car door. It feels cool against my skin.

"What else do you wanna do?"

"To get to hell outta here."

"So what's stopping you?" he asks again.

"You like that question, don't you?" I laugh.

"Well?"

"Me," I say again.

"And you like that answer," he concludes with a shy smile. He looks almost cute in the twilight, with the moon buffing his long face and cropped mocha-brown hair. "And I want a black scorpion."

"A scorpion for a pet?" I wrinkle my nose.

"Hell yeah."

"I think you've been in too many mosh pits," I say with as much affection I can muster for somebody who thinks a black scorpion is good company.

"Man, you should try it sometime...do some head-banging."

"How long have you known me, Fred?"

"Feels like forever."

"And you think Molly Dorman and a mosh pit are a good fit?" I hear my laugh bounce around the lake and startle night birds in the blowing grasses.

"I think you and I are a good fit," he whispers, keeping his head down and his hands stuffed into his Levis. I don't know what to answer him. The last thing I want to do is hurt his feelings, but we've been down this road so many times that I think that he will never take no for an answer.

"I enjoyed your last letter," I say, changing the subject. "I could just see you on that beach."

"Puerto Rico is great. The rum is the best part."

"How's your mother doing?" I ask, also avoiding the mere mention of booze.

"Crazy," he says matter-of-factly. "Your Dad?"

"Crazy," I say just as matter-of-factly, though I've never

Prima Donna Sunshine

told Fred any details. He doesn't even know that Dad's an alcoholic. It's easier just to sum it up by saying that he's just nuts.

Twilight is splashed with stars. Sapphire blue lingers over the fields and then sinks into indigo. I imagine mixing a palette that would capture its transparency. "I'd better get back," Fred says reluctantly. "I've been home for a couple days and really haven't spent any time with my mother. I'll never hear the end of it." He looks at me and smiles. "I like your hair, by the way. It's gotten really long."

"Thanks." Fred brushes my arm and leans in for a kiss, a kiss that feels like a feather against my mouth. "Fred, you mean a lot to me, but you know where I stand…I'm sorry," I say gently, as if soft words will blunt the edge of the truth. He nods, avoiding my eyes. He looks like a little kid who just got into trouble. His childish mannerisms are both endearing and worrisome, and I wonder what's happened in Fred's life to make him so oddly sheepish even after serving in Operation Desert Storm and being in the service for years.

We get into my car. Uncomfortable silence between us hangs heavy as my tires kick up a cloud of dust; it swirls like blue smoke in the moonlight.

I want to reach out to Fred as I drive him home, but he's lost in his own orbit. "See ya," he says as soon as I come to a stop.

"Fred…" He gets out and turns around to grab his jacket from the back seat. Our eyes meet briefly, long enough for me to notice a tear burning down his face. He shuts the car door and sprints into the house. I pause before backing up, until I see the light turned out over the front porch.

"Nice to meet you," I say to Peg, The Old Bitch's new driver and companion. She's standing in our doorway as she looks me up and down.

"I see we got a redhead on the job," Dad comments when he notices Peg's ginger curls. He's surprisingly cheerful.

"Looks like you've got your own redhead," Peg answers with tongue-in-cheek as I stand aside so she can come in. I shut the door to keep out the sweltering heat and wonder what bug crawled up her ass. At least I know that my latest henna treatment turned out as I'd hoped. "I just wanted to meet you, Tom, and ask you where I should park when Mrs. Bosco is at her sculpture class. It's a maze around that part of the city."

"Most of the time, I just went somewhere else or drove around until she was done," Dad replies, getting up to pour himself more seltzer. It's good to see him finally getting around without the wheelchair.

"Great." Peg sighs with sarcasm. I shudder to think what The Old Bitch has told her about us.

"Good luck," Dad says to her.

"I'm gonna need it," she says. "The woman's crazy." She sure doesn't beat around the bush.

"Got that right, but she means no harm," Dad says.

"How'd you take the screaming?"

"Just listen to the traffic reports and let her bounce," Dad advises.

And get stone drunk when you go home, I'd like to add.

"Well, take it easy," Peg says and sees her own way out.

Dad goes to the bathroom while I hunt through the fridge to figure out what to make for dinner.

The artist next door has gone away for a few days, and apparently left his three dogs chained outside in their yard. A neighbor comes to feed them very day, but the barking doesn't stop after she leaves.

I have dinner halfway finished by the time Dad saunters out from the bathroom. He looks distracted. "You okay, Dad?" I ask.

"Fine." I can tell he's lying. He does what he always does when he lies; he wrinkles his nose like a five year old with a cold. Once. Twice.

"You sure?" I ask again as I fluff a steaming bowl of kasha. "I'm fine. For chrissake, leave me alone."

He's been driving again, short distances, and getting his strength back. The wheelchair is tucked away in storage. My classes will resume in the fall at one of the girls' houses.

I have at least half a life now that Dad's sober. I got in touch with two friends from high school, and they plan on coming over soon. All seems well, but my gut doesn't feel right. Tom Dorman is too damn happy lately. And that means only one thing.

"No, Baby. You're wrong. Tom would never go back to booze after what he's been through," Mama says when I approach her with it.

"You want to make a bet?" I fold my arms as I lean against the fridge in the Bosco kitchen.

"It's normal to expect it, to even be paranoid," she says as she removes beef tongue from a steaming pot.

"Yuck," I say, turning my head.

"The Old Bitch loves it." I watch her put it on a plate and go about peeling the skin from the meat. "That and broiled lamb chops cooked until cremated."

"Yes, I remember that well," I mumble as I rummage through the pantry to sneak pieces of imported Israeli orange peel dipped in dark chocolate. "I remember that time The Old Bitch chewed a piece of lamb, decided it was too tough and then stuck it right in your mouth so you could see for yourself."

"Crazy bitch," Mama says, cutting the tongue into quarter inch slices.

"And you're crazy for putting up with it. You think that woman Peg would put up with it?" I ask between mouthfuls of bittersweet.

"Honey, I put up with it because I have to."

"I don't know about that," I say. "I've been thinking about how much energy you and I have spent over the past seven years trying to keep the roof over our heads and Dad out of the gutter or six feet under."

"And?"

"Getting out of here and starting a new life somewhere

would probably have taken half the effort, without the agony."

"You don't know what it's like out there, Molly. The rents and the economy are nothing to sneeze at. Tom and I should never have sold the house in Pennsylvania. That was our first mistake. We had nothing to fall back on." Mama spreads the tongue on a platter and seasons it with herbs and spices until it looks like the finest gourmet presentation.

"Well, we do now. We've got that twenty grand in the bank. Dad's supposedly sober and getting on his feet. Let's get out of here. We can make a fresh start somewhere else."

"Give your father a few more months. I just want him stronger before we leap into another life."

"Does The Old Bitch know you might leave?"

"I'm taking one day at a time, Baby."

"Well, I'm thinking of doing something different," I confess.

"You wanna pay rent and work your ass off?"

"I was thinking of being a live-in nanny somewhere. Maybe renting a space downtown where I can sell some paintings and hold classes on the side."

"You wouldn't have time to write," Mama says, busying herself so I can't see the sadness on her face.

"I wouldn't be far, in the area. Probably New Blair."

"Don't worry about me. Just make sure you do what you want. It's long overdue," she says and looks up with a smile. "Wanna taste some?"

"I don't think so."

"Come on, live a little." She hands me a slice of tongue, and I put it in my mouth waiting to gag. I lift an eyebrow. "You like it!" Mama laughs.

"I never thought…" I go back for another slice.

"Never say never, Baby."

"I guess you're right," I say as I make my way down the long metallic hallway to the Bosco's bedroom.

"What are you looking for?" Mama asks.

"Just moseying around," I mumble as I inspect The Old Bitch's vanity. It reminds me of being fourteen when I'd come over to visit Mama when The Old Bitch was out. I'd sit at her vanity and pretend to be the lady of the house.

I see that she still wears Coty dusting powder and uses Clinique cosmetics. Her perfumes Adolfo, Joy, and White Linen still tempt my nose, and I take a sniff of each.

Some of The Old Bitch's jewelry hangs on a crystal-studded knob, and I notice my old favorite—a two carat diamond encased and suspended in a glass square the size of a large sugar cube.

My attention gets snagged on my own reflection in the mirror. I hate my face more than ever, especially my mouth. Mama says I have the Cupid's bow of a silent film star. I say I look like a child.

Fourteen was good; mirrors weren't enemies; poetry flowed; and there was still room for silliness.

I think silliness can cure more ills than medicine. Maybe one of these days I'll be able to evict the ninety year old woman inside me and feel young again.

Prima Donna Sunshine

Summer insects are hissing, thousands of them in the trees and the fields, as I sit on the porch at the Bosco cabin. Mama and Dad are inside watching an old movie as I try to spy on the artist next door. In the darkness, his studio seems to float out of the black and hover over the fence that divides his property and the Boscos'.

I've fallen into the habit of watching him, though I can't see much, only his moving silhouette against bronze light. Sometimes he paints until after midnight, and I can hear the faintest strains of Bob Marley.

I listen to the sounds as the witching hour closes in around me. I try to forget the sick apprehension in my bones and dream that it's my studio behind the Japanese maples. I imagine that it's my life beyond the fence, with someone to love, a noisy house and a patina Buddha outside the glass doors.

Last night, a cold fear gripped my insides while I tried to sleep. My muscles felt paralyzed and encased in ice. I was aware of that old Native woman I had seen at the woman's retreat two years ago; I felt her standing by my bed keeping watch as if Death waited outside the door.

Prima Donna Sunshine

22

My old high school friend Gwen has just bought a townhouse near Bethlehem, and Cindy was married three years ago to the guy she started dating when I quit school. They caught me up on their lives as we all feasted on my Moroccan tagine and Indian eggplant in my downstairs apartment.

We sat around the driftwood table laughing about our school days. Gwen reminded me about the stories I'd write for the girls in our circle, those lurid tales with long sex scenes about boys they liked and couldn't have. Each week they'd receive a new fantasy neatly folded and tucked into their history books. Sometimes Cindy would open one of them during class, and I'd watch her eyes widen as she got lost in a story that would practically give her a rug burn just by reading it. One time the teacher confiscated it, and

Prima Donna Sunshine

Cindy and I almost passed out from fear. We waited in a panic until class ended and Mr. Rawlings handed it back to her. I figured there must have been an angel with a soft spot for teenage stupidity looking out for us.

I could tell that both Cindy and Gwen thought I've been living a cushy, perhaps frivolous artist's life all these years on the Bosco grounds. They left with an air of indifference as they walked past my paintings and writing desk, unaware that Hell can sometimes wear a beautiful mask.

After weeks of observing Dad's almost too nice behavior and Mom's refusal to believe that he's drinking again, I took matters into my own hands. I trailed Dad when he told me he was going to the store to pick up a newspaper.

Two minutes later I was parked next to him in front of the liquor store at the strip mall. I calmly rolled down my window and stared at him. "I was just thinking about it...I'm not doing anything," he protested with a red face.

"Dad, I know you're drinking again."

"I'm not. I swear it."

"Stop lying to me!"

"All right, all right. Just a little bit, to calm my nerves. That's all it's been, a little bit."

"All those trips to the bathroom and holding onto that coffee mug for dear life...I knew it."

"Don't tell your mother! God dammit, don't tell your mother!"

My mouth was dry as cotton as I walked by his car and into the liquor store. He got out and followed me, and I waited by the door to see what he'd do before carrying out my plan. With balls of brass, he picked out a bottle of cheap vodka and proceeded to the counter. I sprang up to the register. "Don't sell him anything!" I pleaded. Two other customers with startled faces snapped their heads around.

"Calm down, I-I'm not buying anything," Dad sputtered.

"If you want to kill him, sell him one more bottle. He's an alcoholic who can't touch another drop, do you understand?" I said to the poor guy behind the counter. He shook his head.

"All right, Miss. Calm down." He raised his palms like he was in a hold up.

"Come on," I mumbled as I grabbed Dad's sleeve and dragged him out of the store. My face burned up with embarrassment even more than his. "I'm sorry, Dad. I had to." Dad nodded and lowered his eyes, got in the Jeep and followed me home.

We avoided each other's eyes for days, and Mama lost it when she found out why. "You crazy son-of-a-bitch!" she yelled, pulling her own hair from frustration. "Do you have any idea what you have put us through? Tom Dorman, why are you killing yourself? I want an answer!" Dad sat on the couch and stared at the floor.

"Shut up," he mumbled.

"There's got to be a reason you want to die."

"I don't want to die."

"Drinking is going to kill you."

"I just want to calm my nerves."

"There are other ways to calm your nerves."

"I don't want to hear it."

"You're gonna hear it, God dammit!"

"Stop screamin', you nasty son-of-a-bitch."

"Tom, how could you? After all we've been through? We could have such a good life now! We've got some money in the bank..."

"Yeah, yeah..." Dad tuned out and turned on the television. Mama started crying. "Where'd they get this Leno guy? How could he replace Johnny Carson?" he asked, keeping his eyes on the news.

"Told you," I said to Mama and then stormed out of the house.

Of course, Dad's found other places to buy booze, and with each sip and each passing day he's managed to undo every shred of progress he's gained with his health.

July feels like Hades. Even with air conditioning and the shade of the cedar trees outside, this wicked humidity creeps into the Bosco cabin.

Dad's sweating bullets as he tries to piss. He's back in the wheel chair, and he's been struggling to urinate for hours. He asks me to hold a bed pan in front of him as he sits in the chair. Bloody drops escape his wilted penis, and he winces with pain. "Come on, Dad, you're going to the doctor." I try to hide my rage. I can't hide my frustration.

I'm impatient, and I grab the bed pan from him when he's finished.

I've turned into a selfish bitch. All I'm thinking about is the heat inside this house, the places where I want to go, and my sanity hanging by a thread.

"Just let me try again later."

"If you still can't urinate within the hour, I'm calling the ambulance."

"Give me one more hour. Th-thanks for helping me," he says. He smiles at me, the smile I remember when I was little. It rips the heart right out of my chest. I pat his back and help him back to bed.

Just as I'm coming out of the bedroom, I hear Zane's Ford Blazer switch gears as it rounds the turn that leads to our driveway. I swallow hard and hope I'm hearing things. I peek out the window. Sure enough, it's him, barreling out of his truck with his jaw clenched. "Who's that?" Dad asks from the bedroom.

"Nothing. I'll handle it," I say, slipping out of the house before Dad finds out that it's Zane.

I know The Old Bitch is home from New York this week, and I pray that she doesn't hear what's coming.

"Hi," Zane says, trying to squeeze a phony smile out of his scowl. I sit on the porch stairs and look at him. My clothes need a wash, and I haven't slept in two days. There's no way in Hell he doesn't notice. He simply doesn't care. "I think it's time you spent some time with your father."

"I'm sorry, Zane, but I'm dead on my feet. Dad's sick again, and I've been up for days with him while Mom works."

"I drove an hour and a half to get here, and I'm not turning back around."

"I had to leave my job with the Donahues. This isn't a joke. He's pissing blood."

"I'm your father. I'm the one who counts." He presses his index finger to his chest with force. His eyes are already blazing.

"He needs me."

"I-eeeee neeeeed you!" he screams, and my ears pop from the volume.

"Stop putting me in the middle!" I scream back with equal force.

"Make a choice! It's him or me, God dammit!"

"I want you to leave, Zane. Right now." I stand up and walk down the steps in bare feet.

"After everything I've done for you!"

"Don't give me that bullshit! What did you ever do for me?" I stomp over to where he's standing and put my finger in his face. "Get out!"

"I gave you everything!"

"Oh, really? You raised me? Supported me? Worked your ass for me like that man in there? You gave me a few dollars, an easel, and a fucking hard time!"

"Fuck you, you little bastard!" Zane slams back into the driver's seat, and I punch the car door as he backs up like a demon. I'm disappointed that he escapes before I can crack the glass. He screeches all the way down the driveway and out to the main road.

I'm shaking so violently I can barely walk up the stairs

and into the cabin. I pray that The Old Bitch and my dream artist next door didn't hear what just went down.

"What's all the screamin' about?" Dad asks when I come back in.

"Zane Davis. I told him off."

"Good, the bum," Dad grumbles from bed. "I'm gonna sleep for a while, ok?" he asks meekly. I can't answer. I feel sick. "Okay?"

"S-sure, Dad," I manage to say as my knees buckle to the living room floor. I cry so hard I wretch as I pull at my hair and my clothes.

After what he's done for me. Does that include making a pass at me?

I claw at my own face. I detest Zane's blood running through my veins.

"Mol-leeey?" Dad asks as I place some ice chips by his bed. "Change the channel for me, will ya?" He points to an invisible television in the corner of the bedroom ceiling. He's officially gone out of his mind. The doctor says it's hallucinations from uremic poisoning.

After Dad failed to urinate for so long, we got him to a hospital, but they accidentally sent him home from the emergency room without a catheter. By the time a nurse inserted one here at home, Dad was delusional from the toxins that had built up in his blood stream. The doctors say we should admit him to the hospital if he doesn't improve in a few days.

I pretend to change channels in the air. "No, not that one. Keep going," he says. I feel insane right along with him as I click two more times like an exasperated mime. "That's good."

"What are you watching?"

"An old movie. Katharine Hepburn."

"That's nice."

I don't know what's worse—Dad thinking that he's watching an old movie or Dad thinking he's seeing old ladies out the window chewing on chicken bones. That was last night's entertainment while Mama and I sat in a stupor of worry and exhaustion.

We got a hospital bed for Dad and put it in the small bedroom upstairs, the same bedroom Rob Bosco and I had made love in four years ago. Its white-washed walls and pale blue window shutters now only remind me of Dad's invalid status.

He's unable to even lift a cup to his lips, so I hold a straw to his blistered mouth. His cheeks look like hollowed-out stone. He lies there in a diaper that we change every few hours while he watches old movies, spies on women chewing on chicken bones, and cheers for the Yankees playing the World Series in the driveway.

The nights are worse. "Ahoy!" he shouts for hours as Mama and I try to sleep. Inside his mind, he's a sailor on the high seas. The Old Bitch, after hearing about it, says that Dad's probably remembering a past life.

All I know is that I pray he hallucinates walking the plank and ten alligators shut him up long enough for us to get some shut-eye.

23

Neil Diamond's black poet's shirt glints with the changing light. The thirteen year old girl in me misses his flashy sequins, but hey, it's 1992, and my troubadour with his acoustic guitar is fifty one.

And I can't scream like I used to, but I give it all I've got as the woman next to me gives me a wink and then lets out a whistle that cuts clear through the deafening applause. I make sure no one is looking and then fiddle with the tape recorder I sneaked in. "Don't worry, look at all the camera flashes going off. No one's stopping anybody from making a memory," Dave says to me. I'm glad I gave him the extra ticket. By the looks of it, he's enjoying the show.

Dave has been a Godsend to Mama and me, even suggesting he drive me to Madison Square Garden tonight. I was glad for the ride as old Blue Eyes is now a few sputters away from being scrap metal. With a hundred-twenty thousand miles on her tough-girl motor, it would be a shame if our last real adventure together was breaking down in the Lincoln Tunnel.

The stage swivels around, and the lights dim to pulsing sapphire. I feel enclosed in an envelope of ten thousand people as Neil sings a song that made me cry as a kid. I lean on the balcony and look down on the stage with binoculars. The drum's steady heartbeat brings tears to my eyes as it did on record eleven years ago. But this time it's not only the music.

My thoughts go out to Dad in the hospital. He's been there for two weeks now with liquid nourishment in his veins. His hollow cheeks are slowly filling in again, and the hallucinations have stopped. Except for one, two days ago when I was there. "What's that ball of light at the foot of the bed?" he asked me.

"Don't know, Dad. How long has it been there?"

"All day."

"Maybe it's an angel," I said, and then took a felt marker on the board over his bed and drew our initials—T, E, and M inside a heart with an arrow through it. It was my private way of thanking whoever's upstairs for Dad's slow recovery.

"When's the concert?" he asked me, completely lucid.

"Two days."

"I wish I could go with you," Dad said.

"Me, too, Dad." He squeezed my hand.

"You know what today is?" Mama asked him. He

thought for a minute and then answered with certainty.

"Our anniversary." He gave Mama a sweet smile before tears dampened his face.

"Why are you crying, Tommy?" Mama stroked his forehead with a gentle hand.

"I loved you so much. You were my God, Emma," he whispered.

"I spent almost my entire life thinking you never loved me," Mama says, crying with him. "Why didn't you ever let me know?"

"I wasn't good enough for ya," Dad answered, sobbing into her shoulder.

The show's over, and I get ballsy. So ballsy, I go right up to the stage and hang around while roadies start dismantling lights and instruments. "Hey, any chance I could say hello to Neil? Been a fan most of my life," I say to one of them. The guy shrugs.

"Sorry, Miss. Not without a backstage pass."

A few seconds later, I notice a young man give me the once-over before he starts putting guitars in cases. He looks a lot like Neil. I wonder if he's a relation. Dave pokes my ribs.

"Go on, ask him. He likes you," Dave whispers. I take a step forward, but nothing comes out of my mouth. "Hurry up, before he leaves." But I stand there as if bound and gagged.

"You should have said something," Dave says on

way out to the parking garage.

"I just couldn't."

"He sure liked you. I'm sure he would have let you backstage."

"What's the use?"

"You've waited years to get a chance to meet the guy, that's why." Dave squeezes my shoulders, part consolation and part "you dumb ass."

"I'm just nobody."

"Molly Dorman, you are somebody and don't you forget it."

The concert was two days ago, and I'm still kicking myself all over town for being a shrinking violet. I'm in Dad's hospital room trying to keep my eyes open. I feel too depressed and tired to live.

Dad is asleep, so I stare at the rain falling like daggers past the window and into the courtyard three stories down. Hurricane Andrew drowns the world as gold street lights quiver through the wall of water. "He didn't wake up all day," Mama says, startling my thoughts.

"Sleep is good. I need some myself," I complain as I flop into a vinyl chair the color of pea soup. I notice that our initials on the board over his bed have finally been erased.

"Mrs. Dorman?" Doctor Anderson says on his way into the room.

"Hello Doc," Mama says with a tired smile.

"Well, looks like Tom's out of the woods and will make

a full recovery. With a few more days of nourishment, he'll be ready to go home." He lifts his bushy eyebrows and makes a notation on his clipboard.

"I never heard more wonderful news, Doc. Thanks a million." Mama shakes his hand. "While you're here, I'm a little concerned that he didn't wake up all day. We've been here for hours."

"I'm sure it's nothing to be alarmed about. They took him down for a stomach test this morning, and the medication takes time to wear off."

"Stomach test? What for?"

"He was complaining of some distress. We found nothing. No worries." Doctor Anderson gives me a smile and then leaves.

"God damn doctors, they can't leave well enough alone," Mama says as she grabs her purse. "Come on, let's head home. We waited long enough for him to wake up."

On our way out, Mama stops at the nurse's station. "Keep an eye on him tonight, will you? He didn't wake up all day. I have a bad feeling," Mama says.

"Go home and get some rest, Mrs. Dorman. We'll keep an eye on things. That's why we're here."

"You better."

The hard rain and wind tapers as we drive home. We're silent, except for Mama's repeated concern, "Honey, I'm worried. Something doesn't feel right. He should have been awake by now."

Prima Donna Sunshine

"You heard the doctor. Dad's out the woods. Relax," I say with impatience. I'm sick of hospital trips, worry, and those damn late summer katydids hissing in the trees.

"Well, at least the rain is stopping," Mama says as we head into the Bosco cabin.

A half hour later the phone rings. I mute the television. "It's probably The Old Bitch," Mama says right before she answers it. Schnapps stirs in his sleep near my feet, and I take a sip of hot chamomile tea.

It's not The Old Bitch on the line. It's Dr. Anderson at the hospital. I hear shards of information splinter around me like falling debris.

Something happened.

An accident.

An overdose of valium.

Five hundred milligrams instead of five.

They gave him Valium this morning, before the stomach test because he was feeling agitated.

Resuscitation attempts for almost an hour now.

They did everything they could.

They never saw someone's heart just stop like that, without even a revived flutter.

Tom Logan Dorman is dead.

Dead.

Overdose?

My mother heard wrong, so the doctor says. He never said anything *like that.*

Out of the woods? He didn't say it quite *like that.*

"They put him to sleep like a dog!" Mama screams

when she hangs up. "And that son-of-a-bitch tells me he never said it! Five hundred milligrams!" Mama's knees buckle, and she tries to hold onto me.

I have no answer. Only a scream that makes the bones in my head rattle from sheer force. A scream that's been cemented inside my body for seven years. In my gut. In my throat. Imploding. Exploding. A sound I never thought I was capable of. "It was all for nothing!" I scream. Blind with tears, I back up toward the front door. "After what we've done to try to save him!" I then hear myself mumble something about going to The Old Bitch's garage, starting the car, and keeping the doors closed. Carbon monoxide. A sure way out of here. "This war was all for nothing! I swear to God, if he's dead, I'm going with him!"

"And let me bury both of you! Molly!" Mama grabs my shoulders and holds me until I can't fight her anymore. "Oh, God, let him go!" Mama cries. "Let him go." She rocks me until I stop shaking, until I can breathe, until I promise not to abandon her. "It's over. It's over," she says as she sobs into my hair; the sound of our grief like a train wailing into the night.

Mama and I sit with Schnapps. We hold him and each other, the three of us curled in a heaving ball with the sound of katydids grinding in the darkness until after midnight.

I imagine Dad on the other side, happy to see his old man.

I imagine Dad slapping his frozen knee, now healed and perfect, and saying, "I finally got rid of that son-of-a-bitch!"

I imagine his face young again with his gold hair waving over his brow.

I imagine him sober.

I go to the kitchen sometime before dawn. I force down a few sips of tea and go into a drawer for a spoon. There amid the utensils, three newly-born mice, hairless and pink, take their first breaths of life.

25

It's noon, and Mama and I are blasted awake by a knock on the front door. We fell asleep sometime around eight this morning after Mama left a message on The Old Bitch's answering machine in New York. "Oh, God, don't let it be her," Mama says as she tries to get up and answer the door. I drag myself out of bed.

Morning is clear as a diamond. Hurricane Andrew headed out to sea and left New Jersey glistening. The birds are singing. "I'll get it, Mama," I say, scuffling to the door. I open it a crack and a shock of sunlight slaps me in the face. I focus on Ada, The Old Bitch's best friend from Hoboken. Her iodine red hair shocks me even more, and I find myself wide awake. I'm standing in my nightgown, and I can only guess that I look like a blow fish from crying all night.

"Dear, I hope I didn't come at a bad time," Ada says. "Mrs. Bosco and I arrived from New York a little while ago. We heard about your Dad." Her eyes are compassionate. "We brought you some food from Zabar's." She holds up two shopping bags filled to the rim.

"So thoughtful," I say. "Come on in, Ada." I stand aside. Mama peeks out from the hallway. She ties her bath robe and puts on a tired smile but bursts into tears as soon as she looks at Ada.

"I know, Emma. I know," Ada says as she rocks Mama against her shoulder.

"Those bastards," Mama whispers. "He just pulled through so they could put him to sleep like a dog," she cries.

"I'm sorry, Emma. For both you and Molly." Ada leads Mama to one of the living room couches, and they sit down. "Molly, there's chicken soup in there and everything we thought you'd need. Just put it in the fridge before it spoils," she says, patting my mother's shoulders.

"Sure," I say as I head to the kitchen.

"Come now, Emma," Ada says. "Mrs. Bosco wants to see you."

"I can't see anyone right now," Mama says flatly.

"You need people around you," Ada persists, and I grind my teeth as I put food away. I know what's coming even before the phone rings.

Mama answers it. "Yes, Mrs. B. I know you're here for us. Thank you," Mama says without emotion. Mama nods her head and from my view, I can see her rolling her eyes and then widening them with disbelief. "What?" Mama asks suddenly. "Mrs. B, my husband just died. I have to make funeral arrangements. No, I cannot come in to straighten things out for you today." I slam down a dish on the kitchen counter right before Mama hangs up.

"Emma, I think it was Rosa's way to get you over there without being overly emotional."

"Don't give me that bullshit, Ada," Mama says with blunt annoyance. "You go back and tell her I'm coming back to work when I'm good and ready."

"All right, Emma." Ada stands up and moves toward the door. She looks shocked. I guess she's used to seeing Mama cater to The Old Bitch's every whim.

"Thank you for the food. Thank Mrs. B for me, won't you?" Mama says, softening the edge in her voice.

"You're welcome." Ada smiles and turns around before she leaves. "Emma," she says.

"Yes?"

"Rosa and I have been friends since we were girls. There's nothing I wouldn't do for her. But I couldn't work for her." Ada looks guilty having said it and adds, "I don't know how you and Tom withstood it for so long. Especially Tom."

"How do you mean?" Mama asks.

"I was with Rosa many times, when he'd drive us places. She'd scream her lungs out all the way there."

"At Tom?"

"Yes. There were a couple of times he pulled over on Route 80 and cried like a baby and pleaded for her to stop."

"Tommy? Crying on the side of the highway?"

"You got it." Ada knits her brows.

"He never told me any of it," Mama says and then starts crying.

"If the man had a problem with alcohol, I'd see how working for Rosa compounded it." Ada sighs. "Listen, you take care, okay?"

"T-thanks, Ada. It means a lot," Mama whispers, choking on tears. Ada leaves, and Mama and I look at each other in silence, both of us imagining tough Tom Dorman pulling to the shoulder of the road and crying.

"Can you imagine the stuff he never told us?" Mama asks. I nod. "That macho attitude of his. He could have just quit this God-damned job instead of becoming a hopeless drunk."

"Maybe he needed the excuse to keep drinking," I say.

"Oh, Tommy! You crazy fool!" Mama yells, shaking her fist to heaven. "Let me know you're okay. Give me a sign!"

We make arrangements with the local funeral home, a simple service led by Nedda from our old church. If Dad was here, he'd laugh knowing that the fumbling organist is now an eloquent minister. We informed people Dad knew, a few business owners Dad had been acquainted with and a few people close to Mama and me at one time or another. We chose wildflowers over gaudy blooms. Dad would like that.

Mama and I both agree that we do not want Zane there.

Or The Old Bitch. Mama asked her to respect her need for privacy at this time. She also told her that her presence would make us even more emotional.

Mama said The Old Bitch seemed happy to be off the hook. She didn't give a rat's ass about my father, and had no inclination to attend his funeral.

Mama and I been sleeping every chance we get, making up for months without deep rest. I've taken Dad's bedroom upstairs. We removed the hospital bed and put back the white wicker bed. The room is small, and the pale blue window shutters invite the morning and afternoon light like a benediction.

Right now, the bed is white-washed with sun, and the breeze from the open windows is perfumed with hosta blooms. It wafts over me as I float on the surface of sleep.

I'm startled when the phone rings. "I thought you unplugged it, Molly," Mama says from the next room over.

"I know I took care of it."

"It must be your phone downstairs."

"I thought I unplugged that two days ago," I mumble, getting out of bed. I head downstairs to my apartment as the phone keeps ringing and ringing. "Hello?" I ask, more than slightly annoyed. The line is dead as a door nail, not even a dial tone. As I put down the receiver I notice the phone cord unplugged from the wall and dangling over the chair right where I had left it two days earlier

"Who is it?" Mama asks at the top of the stairs.

"Dad, giving you your sign," I say, smiling and holding in a storm of tears.

Prima Donna Sunshine

"He looks too pale," Mama whispers to me in the funeral home vestibule.

"He's dead," I say.

"Tommy always had a pink complexion," Mama says as she rummages through her purse for her make-up bag. She finds the powdered blush. "Let me know if anyone comes," she adds before scampering back to the viewing room so she can touch up Dad's face.

She comes back two minutes later with a laugh stifled by tears. I take a deep breath. "Do you want me to come with you?" she asks.

"No. I have to do this alone," I say, giving her a hug. "I love you, Mama."

"I love you, Baby."

Dad's handsome in his favorite Navy blue jacket and a cornflower blue shirt we bought especially for his final social engagement. Mama's added blush to his face looks natural. So natural, Dad simply looks asleep.

I can barely focus as I reach to touch his folded hands. They feel like cold cement. No part of him yields to my touch—hands, chest, or cheek—as I stare at the shell of Thomas Logan Dorman and wonder where his spirit has flown.

His obituary says he leaves behind a wife and a daughter. It doesn't say that he died in a war against himself, and he almost took us with him.

I lean my weight against his coffin as obsessive thoughts twist my insides. I find myself boiling with rage when I think about trying to locate Dad's hospital records. Mama was incapacitated with grief, so I handled it. Two times I was sent away because the person at the hospital in charge of records of the deceased was not there. Yesterday, on my third attempt, they sent me down to the hospital basement, past the morgue and finally, the area of defunct files. "May I help you?" the woman asked, lifting her eyes over her reading glasses to inspect me.

"My father died unexpectedly three days ago, and I was told I can locate his records here."

"I'm sorry, Miss. This area is only accessed by appointed hospital employees."

"Yes, and that would be you, correct?"

"Why do you want to see records of the deceased?" She knitted her brows with annoyance.

"I have a right to see my father's records."

"I'm sorry, I cannot help you."

"I need to see his records. His name is Thomas Dorman, and he died on August eighteenth."

"Miss, you are wasting my time and your own. I don't know who sent you down here."

"This is sick," I said before storming down the hall to the elevator. Had I remained one second longer, my fist would have relocated the woman's reading glasses to the other side of her head.

Last night Mama sat me down with a pained look. I knew right then and there that Emma Dorman the perpetual doormat was getting cold feet. "Anderson and everyone at that hospital is going to dig up Tom's past, the booze, everything. They're going to drag his name through the mud. We have to consider that before we go ahead with a lawsuit." She started crying.

"Mama, everyone knew anyway. It's not like this big secret, even though we talked ourselves into believing that," I argued.

"My beautiful girl, I don't want all of this getting on you."

"What's the difference? I think we're already covered in mud."

"We have a snow ball's chance in Hell of winning. It's like trying to sue God."

"They overdosed him, Mama! And what about the other hospital where they sent him home without a catheter? They're both responsible!"

"It won't bring him back," Mama whispers. "It won't bring my Tommy back."

"We should have requested an autopsy."

"His body has been through enough." Mama started crying again, uncontrollably. "I'm so tired of fighting."

I look at Dad's dead face and try to reconcile with Mama's decision, at least for tonight.

Oddly, only beautiful memories come, one by one in radiant colors like untended roses in front of an abandoned house. Roses gone wild with thorns and beauty.

"Miss Dorman, I don't mean to disturb you," Jason, the funeral director says, breaking my reverie. "I just want you to know that some people have arrived. I won't let them proceed until you are ready." His smile is comforting, and I return it.

I turn back to Dad and kiss his granite forehead. "Be free, Daddy. I love you."

Dad never read anything I had ever written, so I wrote something for him in hopes that he's listening now. I sit in the front row next to Mama and my darling Patty who has flown in from Hawaii. I squeeze their hands as tears finally come like a broken dam.

The Dad I had for twenty-three years was a complete stranger to me. Sure, I know that he loved deep-dish pizza, hated soup and vegetables, and chose to take sewing instead of shop when he was a boy in Junior High. I know that he believed in aliens, ghosts and mind power, knew Latin and could recite Shakespeare. I know that he liked Jim Croce's music and wore Brut cologne. I know that he played the harmonica once in a while and could have been good enough to play on one of Mama's recordings had he practiced a little more. I know he idolized Charles Lindbergh, and his favorite film was Casablanca.

I don't know if he truly believed in God or if he prayed. I won't know what he thought about human rights or abortion. I don't know what he thought about Capital punishment or war.

I don't know why he was like barbed wire to anyone who came too close. I don't know if he was ever happy in his seventy years on this earth.

Prima Donna Sunshine

I don't know if he knew I loved him.

I don't know if he loved me.

Thomas Dorman goes to his requested cremation and eternal rest an unknown, elusive man.

Dad, I tried everything. I gave you my soul, a self I will never be again, even my hatred. I know it was not enough to conquer that black wave inside you. None of it was enough. But it was all I had. It was all I had.

26

Jean, Dr. Anderson's nurse, left a message on our answering machine. She's the tall one; the one who takes blood pressure and weight at Anderson's private practice and always has a good joke on hand.

She's also the one who had a king-size crush on Dad. "Emma, I heard about what happened at the hospital," Jean said with a hushed tone. "Call me. I have to speak to you," she added before hanging up.

Mama called her back the next day, and Jean suddenly acted as if she just wanted to express her condolences. Mama said that it couldn't have been more obvious that the woman had been silenced.

Dad's ashes will arrive today or tomorrow. Even if Mama changes her mind about taking action against the hospital, there is no possibility of chemical evidence after cremation.

Mama has fought a long battle with Dad, and she's so ashamed of the whole ordeal, I can understand why she cannot face a court trial.

I also surmise that The Old Bitch's influence hasn't helped. "Emma, if you file a case against that hospital, I'll kill you!" she said to Mama more than once this past week, adding, "Emma, won't it be wonderful, just the two of us going into our old age together?"

Mama knows that The Old Bitch doesn't want her to get any real money or she'd be out of this job in a heartbeat. Mama just nods and secretly plans her escape. But I'll believe it when I see it.

I'm trying to figure out what my life boils down to now that I'm no longer sucked into Dad's orbit. I know I cannot resume teaching, not yet anyway. I feel as if I've just come back from a war and putting one foot in front of the other on familiar ground is almost too unsettling to bear.

My position at the Donahues has dried up since they hired another cook. Christine said she held out as long as she could; I can't blame her. I heard through the grapevine that a local nursing home may be looking for an activities director sometime before Christmas. Perhaps I'll find my equilibrium enough to apply for the job.

For now, I'm taking one day at a time, and today I plan on pulling out my journal and those three hundred and twenty-one pages of unfinished manuscript. Words are crowding my brain, even in my sleep.

Right now I'm on my way back from picking up peaches from a nearby farm. Before I left the house, I noticed the artist next door throwing a ball around with his kids. So much for my fantasies of him all these months. Pot belly, crew cut, short temper, and big feet with bunions wasn't exactly what I had in mind.

I head down country roads and notice yellow leaves on the trees. I open the car windows to let in the last traces of August as I have a good cry. I've been holding in what feels like a tornado since Dad died. I know that Mama is dangling by a fragile thread under her calm exterior. I'm afraid she might lose it if I show the magnitude of my own grief and find myself pushing down a fist full of tears all day long. I fight it by leaving the room, deep breathing, punching a pillow, or slapping my face if I have to.

Anything that will dam up what might never have an end if I ever let it out.

I drive along one of my favorite country roads with one hand on the wheel while I bite into a peach as big as a baseball. A gush of sticky juice spills over my cheeks, down my chin, onto my chest and into my denim lap. I pull over and grab a handful of tissues from the glove box. I get out of the car laughing. I'm glad to see that I'm the only one on this lonely road as I finish the peach with a sense of glee.

I can't stop laughing, as if all the tears I've corked have fermented into a strange elixir. My senses throb with clarity. Colors shimmer, even the purple heads of the thistles pricking the scented air with their spines. Swallows brush their white bellies over the fields as they rise and fall in flight, their silver notes swirling inside my ear drums.

Earthy attars of goldenrod, clover, and sun-dried grasses waft under my nose.

Without a shred of logic, I catch an updraft of unexpected and unreasonable euphoria. I have never felt more alive.

Zane must have received my note about Dad's death because here he is, parked in our driveway. It doesn't matter that I requested space for both Mama and me. As usual, nothing matters but his own feelings. "I can't believe that old bull is gone. Tom, you old devil," Zane cries as Mama sits in his car and consoles him. I listen from my bedroom window and roll my eyes. Zane can sit out there and cry until dawn for all I care. I don't want to see him.

A half hour later, he comes inside with Mama. "Molly?" he says until I feel I have no choice but to answer. His voice is cracked with grief. I shuffle out to the living room, and he grabs me in a hug. "I loved Tommy. You might not believe that, but we went back a long way." He caresses my hair. "I need you and your Mama. Life is too short, Honeychild. Let's put it all behind us. Can we?" He pulls away from me and touches my cheek. "When I was in the war, on the islands, sometimes I'd collect scorpions in a jar and shake them, just for the hell of it. You know what happened?" he asks. "They turned on each other. I think that's what happened to all of us the past few months. It's what happens when humans have no way out." He searches my eyes. It crosses my mind to spit in his face and tell him to shove a few scorpions up his ass. If I had taken after him, it's exactly what I would do.

But it's clear that I am my mother's daughter, after all.

The three of us form a circle, leaning on each other for support as we give each other space to grieve. Zane weeps, and it doesn't take long for Mama and me to overflow, too.

I wonder how Zane can cry for a man whom he envied sometimes with murderous passion. I wonder how Mama can mourn the husband who maimed her self-worth with infidelity and near-psychopathic coldness. And I wonder how I can mourn a father who gutted my soul, year after year, with his words as well as his silence.

Each of us has earned the right to not waste another tear or regret on Tom Dorman. Yet we tighten the circle and despite all, choose love.

Every second in this world, something ceases. A heartbeat, a fire, a belief. We go through life prolonging and fearing it, but perhaps death is simply the birth that ends all deaths.

Maybe it's inevitable that we all make a hash of it in this world. Maybe it's just one big, crazy psych ward where we come to grow, hurt each other and then graduate. Maybe in the end, one way or another, we will realize that we've hurt ourselves the most.

Perhaps death is a gentle and merciful old woman, her sterile hands mending all shattered things, even souls. Tonight I can almost hear her voice. She sings in our tears and the laughter between. A low and rhythmic chant of redemption that is soft as snow on a raven's wing.

Pigs must be flying. Emma Dorman quit her job.

The Old Bitch had called Mama in to work knowing well that it was Christmas morning. The Old Bitch threw a candy box at her simply because Mama asked her if she should gift-wrap the presents on the coffee table. When Mama turned around to leave, The Old Bitch lost it and grabbed Mama by the hair until she got her onto the floor. From what Mama tells me, it was a cat fight worthy of a daytime soap. Before she left, Mama shook The Old Bitch by the wrists like a vicious cat that had swiped her one time too many. She also told her that she's going to die a very lonely old woman.

The Old Bitch said she wanted us out within forty-eight hours, but when Mama mentioned the words *lawsuit* and *physical assault*, the greedy Old Bitch ended her threats in a heartbeat.

We've spent a week looking frantically at every rat hole from here to the Poconos, but we think we're finally onto something worthwhile, a one-bedroom basement apartment just outside of town. "We'll put more things in storage, that's all," Mama says with optimism when I ask how we're both going to live in such a small place. "You take the bedroom so you have room to write and paint. We'll buy a futon and I'll sleep on it in the living room."

"Oh no you're not!"

"Yes I am. I'll be happy with my bookcases and away from that bitch. Come on, keep your mind open."

"Okay, okay," I grumble as we pull into a circular driveway. The house is Colonial blue, right on the road, with a ton of land in the back.

"The landlord sounds nice, originally from Brooklyn, too. And his wife's an artist," she adds.

"Sounds good. Just as long as the tub doesn't look like the black lagoon like the last one we looked at."

"Have a little faith, Molly Dorman." She tugs my hair as we ring the doorbell.

"Come on in," a dark-haired woman says as she takes a drag on her cigarette and stands aside to let us in. She calls to her husband in the kitchen.

"Hi. I'm Joe," he says, extending a warm hand to each of us. His hazel eyes are soulful, and his features are pleasant with terra cotta skin and salt and pepper hair.

"Hi Joe," Mama says with a smile, and I follow suit.

"And this is my wife Magdalena."

"Don't call me Magdalena!" she snaps, and Joe's face blushes into an innocent smile.

"That's your name, isn't it?" he asks her with the expression of a smart-ass fifth grader teasing a classmate.

"Call me Maggie," she says to us. Joe chuckles.

"Come on downstairs, and I'll show you the apartment," he says. "I don't know if you like to walk or bike, but the three acres out in the back lead down to a river trail."

"Sounds wonderful," I say as we all make our way downstairs to a humble haven with a pretty glass door, eat-in kitchen with a yellow sink, a big bedroom, and nice size living room.

"How much?" Mama asks.

"Six hundred, includes all utilities."

"Tom's Social Security check covers it," Mama says to me. I nod.

"So where did you work before?" Joe asks Mama.

"At an insane asylum," she answers, and we all laugh.

"Sounds too familiar," Joe says. "I work for the Government, the post office." He rolls his eyes and mumbles *Mother* in Italian.

"Actually, my late husband and I were caretakers for a wealthy couple. The old man died three years ago. He was a doll, but the wife…"

"How about you, Molly?" Joe asks.

"She's a writer and an artist," Mama interjects, putting her arm around me.

"Magdalena's an artist, too. Notice the paintings in the living room when you go upstairs."

"Sure." I smile, and Joe returns it warmly. "I have two interviews for a day job. One, as a private cook and the other, an activities director at the nursing home. We'll see," I add.

"I started out wanting to be a sculptor, but it wasn't in the cards," Joe says, smoothing his mustache and then folding his arms casually.

"It's a tough business," I reply.

"It is tough. I ended up going to Seton Hall and getting a degree in finance. The only trouble is that I couldn't see myself getting on that train to New York every day and living for the bottom line."

"How'd you end up in the post office?" Mama asks.

"I noticed the postman outside our door one day and decided I wanted a job that I didn't have to take home with me. First day on the job I learned that the guy next to me was a chemist and another had a master's degree in finance. I figured I wasn't the only nut," Joe says with a laugh. "I've met all kinds—rich, poor, crazy, interesting. I could write a book about the people I've met on my route over the past twenty-five years."

"Why don't you?"

"I thought about it. Maybe someday. I wrote one about my grandfather years ago."

"I'd love to read it. Did you get it published?" I ask.

"Nah, tried a few things and then set it on the back burner. What do you write, Molly?"

"Fiction and poetry. I've been getting back into it. It's taking me awhile to get in the groove again," I lament. "Enough about me, Mama's an incredible songwriter." I smile and put my arms around her shoulders.

"No kidding!" Joe says. "Sell any songs, Emma?"

"Came close so many times it's embarrassing," Mama says with a laugh and then turns to me. "What do you say, Baby?" Mama asks. "Do you see us living here?"

"I'm game if you're game," I say.

"We'll take it, Joe," Mama says with delight.

"Do you think it's enough room for the two of you?" Joe asks.

Prima Donna Sunshine

"We'll make due," Mama says with optimism.

"Great. When do you think you can move in?" he asks.

"Can we start bringing stuff over tomorrow?" I ask Joe.

"You bet," he answers with a sweet smile.

Mama writes out a check as security. Joe takes it and says, "It'll be nice having you both here. I can tell you're good people."

We go upstairs, and I study one of Maggie's paintings hanging above the couch. Her careful brushstrokes portray an early morning fisherman leaning into his boat on a misty riverbank. "I like your lighting," I say.

"Lighting is everything. What is art without light?" she asks.

"Magdalena, Molly knows. She's an artist," Joe says, almost anticipating the fall out.

"I told you not to call me Magdalena!" she snaps again and takes a sip of beer as Wheel of Fortune winds up for the night. She's a pretty woman, and I wonder why she wears such huge glasses on the bridge of her nose. Not to mention those tan slacks that are hemmed too short, exposing white sneakers and three inches of tube socks. She looks like a she's prepared for a record flood.

"I'll see you out," Joe says, stifling a chuckle.

"So, are we going to be neighbors?" Maggie asks.

"You bet," Mama says cheerfully.

"Good," Maggie decides then postscripts it with a smile.

"You take it easy now," Joe says as we leave.

"Thanks. We'll see you tomorrow," I say.

We don't know how long we'll be here in this apartment, but it sure feels good to be free of The Old Bitch. Mama and I are cleaning houses to cover the rest of our expenses until something better comes along.

I got the position at the nursing home, but something happened on the third day that I still can't figure out. All I know is that the walls started closing in on me while a wave of nausea sent me outside to get a breath of air. "You look like you've just seen a ghost. You all right, Child?" one of the nurse's aides asked me. I insisted I was okay, but I still couldn't stop the sensation of a live current rippling down my spine and twisting my stomach. I left for the day when the room started to spin and the furniture moved like chess pieces.

Maybe I did see a ghost. Maybe the sight of hospital beds and wheel chairs hit a nerve. Maybe the man in room twenty-five reminded me a little too much of Dad with his catheter, sunken cheeks, and unresponsive eyes.

Whatever it was, I knew I could not go back.

The family in need of a private cook said they had some financial setbacks but will be in touch this coming summer. I plan to follow up. It sounds like a decent job while I focus on writing.

Joe has become a fast friend to both Mama and me. Every other day he comes downstairs to see us, and he stays for an hour or so on Monday nights after Maggie leaves for Bingo. Sometimes the three of us sit in the kitchen and talk about everything from art to UFOs.

A foot and a half of snow is expected to accumulate

today, and I'm hoping that Mama and I will be snowed in tomorrow so we won't have to clean our usual Monday houses. One woman is a fanatic and expects us to clean out and wash her encrusted refrigerator for the same ridiculous amount of money. The other woman, two streets away, is flat-bottomed as a boat, collects anything related to ducks, and wants us to scrub the cracks between her kitchen tiles with a toothbrush. We call that one The Duck House.

I zip up my flannel-lined denim coat, tuck in my messy hair into a hat, and head out for a walk before the snow gets too deep. It's already halfway up my knee-high boots. Joe is shoveling our walkway and whistling a tune from a zany television commercial. His face is somewhere under a waterproof hood. All I can see is the tip of his nose and his black mustache that lengthens when he melts into a smile. "Hi Joe," I say as I walk by.

"Hey Kid, how's everything going?" He stops and leans on his shovel.

"I thought I'd take a walk before it gets too bad out here."

"My best advice is to take the side trail if you want to avoid the drifts."

"Sounds good."

"Have you been following the Nancy Kerrigan and Tonya Harding craziness?" he asks.

"It's awful. I swear the world's getting crazier by the day."

"I have almost three decades on you, and I can say it's

always been crazy. Eh, what can you do? Just keep painting. From what I've seen, you're good, Kid."

"Thanks, Joe. I appreciate it." I give him a wave as I head down the side trail.

I hear the chatter of ravens somewhere in the trees and the sound of snow crunching under my rubber soles as I trek down to the brook. Large rocks sport downy white bonnets. The stream gurgles its way to the river as snowflakes pirouette into dark water, merging and becoming something else. I like to think that humans do the same thing, just with a lot more resistance.

It's good to be here in this sanctuary of wood and water, where falling snow smothers the wild fires inside me, fires no one will ever likely know. Maybe the years will cover and transform them the same way snow pardons a soiled and imperfect world.

27

Mama and I walk into each day as if we're on parole. We inch away from the past, terrified to trust this scarred freedom.

Mama has been spending time at the recording studio with Joni and Lance to work on more demos. I'm glad she's using some of that money in the bank for her music. The hospital bills have eaten up a good chunk of it. What a crock. I can't believe Mama still pays those bastards for killing Dad and getting away with it. It makes me crazy.

I've taken my old manuscript apart and started from scratch. I hope to finish it within a few months and send out a book proposal. Whatever the outcome, I am thrilled to create worlds on the page again.

I've done a few paintings, nothing special, just a few landscapes to stay in the groove. I've asked Joe if he'd sit for me to do his portrait, but he squirms at the mere thought of it. "My nose would take up the whole canvas," he jokes. I tell him that his Italian nose begs to be painted. And his beautiful soul.

Dad's ashes remain in the box they came in. Covered with crimson velvet, they are now a foundation for my prayer altar. He rests beneath lotus beads, sandalwood, and a picture of Baba Muktunanda. The presence of his ashes is now taken for granted until I move them to clean. Last time I accidentally jostled the box, and the side panel popped out along with Dad's heavy bag of ashes. I had expected them to be fine like beach sand and was shocked to see nothing but rough chips of bone. I felt faint as I shoved them back in the box and covered them with the cloth.

Mama still cries daily, but she exudes a peace I haven't seen since I was very small. Her sense of resolution also comes from the fact that she saw Dad a few weeks ago when we pulled into the driveway. She said he was standing on the walkway that leads to our apartment. "Tommy!" she said, rushing out of the car toward him. She said he was wearing dark brown slacks and his tan jacket, the one with the hole in the left pocket. His hair looked gold under the light by our front door, and he smiled at her before disappearing into the darkness. She stood in the driveway and cried from joy.

She also finds comfort in giving his clothing to a few needy people. Last week she gave a homeless man Dad's gray winter coat. I think Dad would like that.

"I don't have to worry about him anymore," she says with a sense of relief, even when she's crying. "All my life I worried about him. I worried about him getting sick, dying, cheating on me, drinking, getting sober, if he was happy or not..."

I feel a sense of relief, too. Mornings are vacant of dread. I pull out my journal from under my pillow when the night's dreams are fresh as wet paint. Sometimes I wake at dawn and feel a rush of words storming my brain the same way poetry came for the first time when I was twelve years old.

Zane has remained a bitter contradiction, loving one week and confrontational the next. Mama and I were all set to visit him and Linda when Zane called and started a nasty fight. He told Mama that he doesn't want us in his life after all and then hung up on her.

After years of trying to make it work with Zane Davis, Mama and I are relieved. Rather than stew over his rabid behavior, Mama and I laughed and popped a chick flick into the VCR.

Dad's anniversary comes hard. Just the mere sound of katydids swarming the dusk makes me sick.

That and something else. I woke up two weeks ago with what I thought was a stomach flu, but it's still hanging on. My nausea is wicked. Just the sound of a cup set down on the kitchen counter can send me heaving. I have cold sweats at night that soak the bed, and I'm so tired I feel like I've done three triathlons in a row.

The doctor found nothing wrong with me and advised a

round of antibiotics. Nothing's helping, not even Mama's trusty homeopathic medicines that have helped me throughout my life with everything from earache to flu. Maggie made me chicken soup and a split pea soup with ham. The soups are delicious, but I can't get more than a spoonful or two past my lips. Mama says I'm the color of ash, and she worries so much I feel guilty for being sick.

Mama and I are supposed to start a new job together after Labor Day weekend. Mama will be doing housekeeping, and I'll be cooking meals five days a week for Dan, a divorced man and his thirteen-year-old son Gregory. They live two towns over in a beautiful big house tucked away in a nook of russet oak trees. I just pray I'll be better by the time we're expected to start.

For now, I just want the neighbor's dog to shut up. She barks furiously for hours at a time. The noise makes my stomach feel like I'm on a roller coaster and keeps me from getting to sleep. Schnapps keeps watch at the foot of my bed and seems to know that his presence makes me feel better. "This too shall pass," Mama says. I pray she's right.

I put a casserole in the oven and lie down on Dan's living room couch. Mom's upstairs vacuuming. I try to get a cat nap before the boy comes home, but it's hard to sleep and keep one eye open worrying about getting caught. I doze off and then the chills come, like ice in my veins. It happens every day, every night, as soon as my head hits a pillow. I shake like there's a live wire inside my spine.

I don't let on to Mama how sick I still feel. She has enough on her plate. All I know is that sometimes I feel so utterly exhausted I either pray to die or get up. It's hard getting meals made, but I manage to pull it off and try to have fun by inventing new recipes to keep myself interested.

The house and property are beautiful here. The light is tinged with burnt sienna from the turning oaks, and deer graze the same time every evening at sundown and the scent of chimney smoke fills the air from the house next door.

There are also plenty of squirrels. One of the little devils stored a stash of acorns in our Jeep and locked in the gear shift. Mama and I came out one night to go home and found that we couldn't put the car in reverse. The crunching sound when we tried to budge it prompted us to investigate, and we made the biggest nut bust in recent history.

Crazy things like that keep us light-hearted. That and the used upright piano we bought for our apartment. It's studio size and perfect until we get Mama's console out of storage after we move into a bigger place someday.

Cindy, my old high school friend is pregnant and expecting a baby girl sometime next year. Sometimes we talk on the phone and vow to get together, but something always comes up and we never get around to it.

Sometimes I fantasize about adopting a child someday if

I ever get my act together. For now, I just want to feel better and finish some writing projects.

All thoughts of finding a lover are dwindling. I can't imagine anyone wanting this worthless heap of bones. Falling in love feels like a big waste of time and energy. Mama says I sound like an old lady. I tell her I feel like one.

1994 arrives with a phone call from Zane. He tells Mama that he's spent the past year succumbing to a relapse of cancer. This time it's in his bones, and he's been on morphine. He has a matter of days left, but he wants to speak to Mama about his art; he doesn't want Linda to know that he's called her. He's so weak he can barely speak and says he'll call back.

"Do you want to talk to him when he calls back?" Mama asks me, coming into my bedroom.

"It ended when he ended it," I say, feeling guilty already.

"You don't owe him anything, Baby," she says, touching my hair.

"I know," I say, trying to convince myself.

"Knowing Zane, he knew he was sick again and didn't want us to see him die."

"Maybe," I say.

The phone rings two days later. I make out bits of conversation as I sit at my writing desk. It's Linda.

Zane died yesterday.

He was nothing but a walking skeleton.

The service will be in Lackawaxen, Pennsylvania, two days from now. Linda would like for us to attend.

Zane's studio is sealed, she emphasizes, and no one is allowed up there.

Mama hangs up and cries. I go into the kitchen and put my arms around her. "Both of those fools are gone," she says. "I loved them both, so differently but equally." She looks up at me. "And I love you, my Baby. Are you okay?" she asks.

"I'm fine," I say, feeling sadness but oddly detached from it.

"Do you want to go to the funeral? Are you feeling too sick?" Mama says.

"I have to go, for my own sake."

Mama calls the florist and orders Zane's favorite flowers—spray roses the color of sunrise, his favorite time of day. She requests one of Zane's quotes, something beautiful and philosophical from his book.

My legs feel devoid of bones as I reach in my closet to pick out something to wear. I realize that I'm twenty-four years old and both of my fathers are dead. There are no more chances-second, third, or tenth, to get it right with either one.

Linda has chosen an extremely religious theme for Zane's service. Like it or not, Zane Davis was an atheist, and he must be turning over already.

It's a small gathering, people from town, friends from his writers group, and a few admirers who collected his paintings or bought his book. Linda sits three chairs away. She is visibly shaken and exhausted despite her Stoic veneer.

I turn my eyes back to Zane. Save for his characteristic nose, he is not even remotely recognizable. He looks like a Holocaust victim. The minister talks about heavenly salvation and reward, and leads us into the Lord's Prayer.

A pianist plays Debussy as a few people go up to Zane's coffin. Mama and I follow. I stare at his hollow, bird-like face and remember the days we spent together. "Thank you for the good times. Most of all, thank you for art," I whisper as I slip a piece of emerald sea glass into his lapel pocket, a small treasure from that trip to Cape May I had saved in a memory box all these years. Mama smiles when she sees my parting gift to him and whispers her own sentiments.

I see the naked symmetry of his bone structure—chiseled nose, cheekbones, and dimple in the chin. So much like mine, yet I feel little paternal connection. I am almost relieved when tears finally come, a quiet and bittersweet rain.

"Try not to worry, Emma. Molly will be okay. There's got to be something they can do." I hear Joe's muffled voice and Mama's concern drifting from the kitchen as I lie

Prima Donna Sunshine

in my bedroom half asleep.

"At least we finally have a diagnosis," Mama says.

"I still don't understand how somebody can be this sick without a definite cause."

"They think Chronic Fatigue Syndrome is viral, but not contagious." She pauses. "I guess that's why a lot of doctors still don't believe this condition is real."

"Yeah, right. Like swollen glands are all in her head." Joe sounds disgusted.

"I worry because they say the majority of patients deal with it for years, even decades."

"Poor kid," Joe says and I can tell Mama's crying. "Try to take one day at a time."

"She didn't need this flu. It's the third one in a couple of months."

"How's the fever?"

"High. If it goes up any further, I'll take her to the ER."

I lie here listening. Joe's voice is a comfort. Sometimes I wonder why Dad and Zane couldn't have been more like him.

The nauseating pain in my muscles has moved from my joints and into my bones. I'm sick of being sick.

Mama's cleaning and cooking now for Dan and his son, and my life's become nothing but these four walls and this bed. I am young, but I'm too exhausted on most days to even walk out to get our mail. I can hardly digest food and bladder-incontinent as an old woman. I barely eat yet I've gained fifteen pounds. I hate myself. Dad was right; I am worthless.

I tune back into Joe and Mama. They're laughing as Mama tells him about the soap opera update to Linda and Zane—how he had removed his signature from all of his paintings so Linda couldn't sell a single piece after he died. "At least she gave us some of his work, and Molly got what she was entitled to," Mama says.

The voices in the kitchen get further and further away as sleep urges me under, but a light in the room jolts me every time I doze off. I thought Mama had turned off the lamp the last time she checked on me. I try to get up to turn it off, but I can only lift my head off the pillow. That's when I realize the light isn't coming from the lamp.

I think I'm hallucinating and blink to clear my vision when I see Dad, motionless and auriferous by my bed. I blink again, but he's still there. He's beautiful and sober. "Daddy?" I whisper, and he reaches out to touch my hair. He doesn't say a word, but I feel love emanating from the rose-gold light that surrounds him; my heart swells and almost breaks. "I love you, too, Dad," I say as my tears choke my words. He smiles before dissolving into the darkness of my bedroom. "Dad..." I whisper again. "Come back. Please come back," I plead, but he's gone. The visitation makes me sob like a baby.

"Molly, looks like your fever is finally going down," Mama says, startling my reverie. I hadn't heard her come into the room. She sits down on my bed and puts her hand to my forehead. "Are you all right, my angel? Have you been crying?"

"I'm fine," I whisper. "Everything's going to be all

right..." I trail off even before I can tell her that Dad was here.

"Sleep, Molly," Mama says. She kisses my cheek then closes the door halfway.

In my mind, I rummage through my bag of memories and take out our mountain nights from long ago. In my dreams I am still a child, and my father is sober. For long, awkward moments, I am a stranger in yesterday's province, a pauper pressing my nose to a window where the light shines gold at twilight.

Then the sound of the whippoorwill breaks across bittersweet fields of remembrance; sleep nudges me under its dark wing, and I am home.

Epilogue

It's simple, really. No big deal. I've done this enough times to not feel nervous, but I do anyway.

It's a familiar sequence. Greet the next person in line, take one of my books from the pile, open the flap, and sign the page as quickly as possible to not hold up the line. Sometimes a person requests that I include their name when I sign a book.

An hour ago someone requested to take a picture with me. I am a published but unknown writer, so it amazed me when it happened.

I'm excited to be here in Philly at Barnes and Noble, but the trade shows are the most fun. The one I attended yesterday was exciting; I was thrilled to learn that Joyce Carol Oates was a few tables away from mine.

I wish Mama was here. At least she got to see my first

book published. Mama never lived long enough to see one of her songs sold, so my getting published when I was twenty-seven was a big deal to her. "To Hell with those songs. My kid's an author! My beautiful Molly," she'd say proudly and then put her arm around me. Sometimes she accompanied me on book signings, and those times were some of the happiest of my life.

I rearrange my books into two piles, one on either side of the table. Sometimes an hour can go by without one person and other times six people line up. "What inspires your books?" is a question I hear often. My answer has changed through the years. I guess it is a sign that I'm growing, and that's a good thing.

Occasionally someone asks me about Chronic Fatigue Syndrome and why I choose to support research for the still-misunderstood condition while other issues loom in importance. "It's important to me," I answer, leaving out the details of the past eighteen years of unpredictable remissions and relapses.

I rummage through my bag so I can check my cell phone for messages but am interrupted by a customer's voice, "Molly Dorman?" I look up and see a woman probably in her early to mid-sixties. She has beautiful, high cheekbones and smiles with hesitance. She must have been gorgeous when she was young, and I wonder how I will look in twenty or so years.

"Yes?"

"You don't remember, do you?" she asks, leaning a little closer. She smiles slowly and picks up a book. Her green eyes spark my memory, and just for a second, I am sixteen years old again, and my heart beats as fast as a hummingbird's wings.

"Kate? Kate Hall?" I ask, already getting out of my chair.

"Oh, can you believe these wrinkles?" she asks with soft laughter. We hug briefly. "I saw the article in the paper about your signing. Good for you, Molly."

"How are you?"

"Remarried now for fifteen years. A good man."

"I'm glad to hear you had a happy ending, Kate." I smile and touch her shoulder.

"I live in Devon, along the Main Line. My kids have kids." She rolls her eyes and smiles.

"A grandmother," I say, shaking my head in disbelief.

"Time sure is a thief," she says with hawk-like observation. "You look well, Molly."

"Thanks. It's been quite a journey."

"A good one, I take it?"

"Let's just say it's been interesting," I say with a laugh, leaving out illness, ten moves, a woman lover, crazy day jobs, and making a hash of it especially after Mama split the scene five years ago.

"Husband? Kids?"

"Husband, yes. Kids, only my books."

"A good man?" she asks.

"A wonderful man, the man I had most admired in the world."

"Where are you living?"

"Well, after living in suburbia too long, I decided to go

home to New Blair."

"I'm happy for you."

"Thanks, Kate." I smile even though I am still in shock that Kate Hall is standing in front of me. Save for those fabulous cheek bones and green eyes, she is very different from the woman who took my breath away so long ago.

"Will you sign a book for me?"

"Of course!" I think for a moment and then open the book flap. I write:

For Kate—remembering our walks and our dreams.

"Thanks, Molly. Good luck." She touches my hand.

"It was so good to see you, Kate." I hand her the book and well up with tears as she proceeds to check-out. I regain my composure before she passes me on her way out of the store. She waves, and I follow suit.

Yes, Time is a thief. It's been nineteen years since Kate and I drifted into separate lives and twenty-seven years since I first saw her through the kitchen window and she'd unknowingly help me get through another day.

Seeing Kate again makes me remember the old days, and I miss my old manual typewriter with the forest green keys. Computers and Kindle, along with turning forty-two last year, have taken a little getting used to.

I tell myself that change is good; technology can be wonderful, and the gray that is coming in gives me even more reason to opt for auburn.

Yet some things never change.

I still love to paint and have a studio I disappear into between novels. I still cook gourmet meals when time and health allow, and I still hope to meet and talk to Mr. Neil Diamond over a good cup of coffee.

And the bad dreams still come at night.

I dream about the hard years that came after I got sick—the welfare office, no help in sight, and not having enough quarters to scrape together to go to the Laundromat. I dream of Mama's dead face in the emergency room cubicle, her features bloated beyond recognition after her heart attack on a cold, rainy Saint Patrick's Day. I dream of bouncing from one place to another—the suburbs of Philadelphia, Washington, D.C.-like a tired bird looking for a place to land.

Mostly, I dream of Dad. In my dreams he's still alive, drunk at the wheel or stumbling into bed. Time heals all wounds, so they say. Year after year the forgetting, the forgiving, the letting go. But drunks never die.

"Any advice for an aspiring writer?" a customer asks, cradling the book when I hand it to her.

"Well, only what another writer once advised me: don't give up and don't have any excuses. Write no matter what."

"Thanks, Molly. It was great meeting you."

"Likewise."

Life's puzzles still elude me, but a few things have come into focus lately. Namely, how some of us can go through life feeling that we are nothing but dirty windows obliterated by mud, and sometimes all it takes is the clean water of someone's love to wash off the filth so the sun can get through.

Our kitchen smells like Mama's during my childhood—garlic and olive oil, rosemary and browned butter, and basil—bright and impossible to forget as the sweet earth of her smile. Dinner simmers in reds of bell pepper and tomato, and muffins rise in the oven. Noah, our little black and white Shih Tzu is curled up in the kitchen keeping a close eye on the food.

Joe comes in from outside and presses me against him. His soft gray hair waves to his denim collar and brushes my cheek. He smells like April and wood smoke. "Hello husband," I say, kissing him and then smoothing his mustache with affection.

"Hello wife," he says as he cups my face in his gentle hands.

"Did you ever think we'd be saying that to each other?" I tease. It's a question I haven't yet grown tired of asking simply because of Joe's response.

"Hell no!" We both laugh.

And I think we're both still in shock.

Four years ago I left the Philadelphia area and headed back to New Blair after a bad break-up. Joe took me in until I got my life back on track. Maggie had lost her battle with cancer six months after Mama died, so Joe and I helped each other to heal the losses in our lives.

No matter who has come and gone in my life, Joe has

remained a constant. He's been landlord, kindred spirit, and anchor in the storm.

He's also turned out to be the unexpected love of my life.

Joseph DiSando had fallen in love with me six months before I fell for him, and he never said a word. We lived in the same house, ate at the same table, and spent more time together than apart, yet he never tipped his hand about his change of feelings or crossed the line on any level. I adore him for that. "I didn't want to upset your life, Molly. You've been through enough," he said later, after I boldly informed him that my heart had tipped over, and my journey all along had led me back to him.

I married Joe on my forty-first birthday; we had a small wedding—seventeen guests, an organic chef, and pink champagne. Joe and I both wore red. Molly Dorman got her older man, after all.

Some people raise eyebrows about the years between us. Some of my lesbian friends have even disowned me because my soul mate turned out to be a man. I'm happy to say that most of the time, people admire our beautiful love story.

I have survived a lot in my time yet feeling worthy of this man's shimmering, unconditional love has been the hardest thing I have ever tried to do.

Every once in a while I take out Mama's demos and sheet music and the song she had written for me when I was a girl. The pages are yellowed by time, but her words etched so long ago strike my heart with new meaning and are like bread during moments of famine.

I feel her right here cheering me on, helping to clean the dirty window. I have come so far, yet some days I am a woman only beginning, having ended so many times.

When my schedule is free and my health is on an upswing, I work as a hospice volunteer or caregiver, and it continues to teach me everything I need to know for the next step along my journey. "There are no lifetimes of happiness, only moments," a one-hundred-year-old lady once said to me as I sat at her bedside. "There are no destinations, only resting places. There is no change, only seasons." I try to remember her precious wisdom and the realization, that in the grand scheme of things, there are no accidents.

I have heard that dying people sometimes see a glowing ball of light at the foot of their beds. Medical professionals believe it is nothing more than near-death hallucinations while others claim it's the light of God or the higher self, waiting to embrace the soul for the journey home.

Dad saw a sphere of beautiful light all those years ago. He wasn't dying at the time and succumbed to an accidental overdose a few days later. It makes me think about—and rethink—the nature of chance.

I also think about the choices Mama and I had made out of love and mostly, fear. Only now can I see what we could have done differently, if only we had loved ourselves.

I realize now that most of my unresolved pain has little to do with my relationship with my fathers—and
everything to do with my relationship with Molly Dorman-

DiSando. I don't know if I will ever get it right, but I am trying.

Whenever I falter, I walk along the river near our house and pick up pieces of driftwood. Each piece reminds me that it once had a soft heart, a lot like mine, which grew wise and beautiful in the harsh womb of the waters. The wood is a survivor of remembrance—burnished and all too human, a life like mine lending its voice to the inaudible.

We are what the wave has made.

About the Author

Marlaina Donato is the author of several books including **A Brief Infinity: Poems**, **The Silver Ladder: Children's Stories for the Magical Years**, and forthcoming titles in Women's Fiction. She is also an accomplished artist and instrumental composer.

Marlaina and her beloved husband Joe live in rural New Jersey.

Prima Donna Sunshine

Made in the USA
Lexington, KY
11 March 2012